Unity AI Programming Essentials

Use Unity3D, a popular game development ecosystem, to add realistic AI to your games quickly and effortlessly

Curtis Bennett

Dan Violet Sagmiller

BIRMINGHAM - MUMBAI

Unity AI Programming Essentials

First published: December 2014

Production reference: 1151214

Published by Packt Publishing Ltd.
Livery Place
35 Livery Street
Birmingham B3 2PB, UK.

ISBN 978-1-78355-355-6

www.packtpub.com

Credits

Authors
Curtis Bennett

Dan Violet Sagmiller

Reviewers
Davide Aversa

Adam Boyce

Jesse Lu

Brent Owens

Angelo Tadres

Francisco Ureña

Commissioning Editor
Akram Hussain

Acquisition Editor
Subho Gupta

Content Development Editor
Prachi Bisht

Technical Editors
Tanvi Bhatt

Siddhi Rane

Copy Editors
Gladson Monteiro

Deepa Nambiar

Rashmi Sawant

Project Coordinator
Sageer Parkar

Proofreaders
Ameesha Green

Jonathan Todd

Indexer
Priya Sane

Graphics
Disha Haria

Production Coordinator
Komal Ramchandani

Cover Work
Komal Ramchandani

Foreword

Artificial intelligence can be one of the most challenging aspects of video game development. Game AI encompasses difficult concepts such as spatial reasoning, pathfinding, movement, awareness, and decision making, all with the goal of combining these concepts into a realistic and lifelike experience for the player. It's no wonder that so many game developers put off AI development to the end of the project. This is a shame, because good AI can make or break the game experience and great AI can make a player fall in love with your game and keep them coming back again and again.

In recent years, AI has become more important than ever. Although the quality of AI in games has increased steadily over time, the results have come more from added attention and effort on the part of developers, rather than from significant breakthroughs in technology. The impact of this is that "good" AI in games has often been limited to projects and teams with large budgets and access to high-end tools. Unity changed the industry by making high-end game development tools available to all developers, big and small. Today's indie developers are creating player experiences that rival those of AAA companies. Until recently, they lacked the tools, knowledge, and know-how to add AI-driven characters that have the same fidelity as the rest of the game. Now this has changed too, with the very best AI tools becoming accessible to every developer.

This book serves an important role in the rise of AI in Unity. In these pages, you will find the guidance, techniques, and examples you need to become a great AI developer. For beginners, the book walks you step by step through the fundamentals of concepts such as pathfinding, patrolling, and creating behaviors for common scenarios such as attacking and crowd movement. You will also be introduced to the numerous tools available for Unity that you'll need along the way. For experienced developers, the book gives you access to best practices, tips, and techniques that will take you from good to great.

I'm incredibly excited about the future of AI and its potential impact on games in the coming years. Game developers are often at the forefront of innovation, and their contributions to filling the world with believable AI will be significant. Go forth, reader, and join the growing ranks of AI programmers!

Bill Klein (aka Prime)

CEO, Rival Theory

About the Authors

Curtis Bennett has been a developer in the games and computer graphics industry for several years. He has worked on developing immersive virtual environments, published research in visual simulation, taught college courses in game development, and worked for various game studios, and he was also an engineer on early versions of the RAIN AI plugin for Unity. Currently, he is the Technical Director for Creative Services at Ideum, which focuses on creating interactive media projects.

> I'd like to thank all the Unity AI plugin developers who make implementing AI with Unity so easy.

Dan Violet Sagmiller has always had a strong passion for game development, although most of his work leads him to senior business development roles. He developed several games, including *Teams RPG*, a space shooter (which won a game development competition at Technology Center of DuPage), and some casual games. He started teaching game development at Heartland Community College in 2005, taking over the existing course and expanding it to six courses. Later, he took a position with Microsoft and expanded the game development curriculum for Bellevue College, including classes on AI, physics, testing and designing using C# and XNA. Later, he moved on to a senior position with Wizards of the Coast, where he also taught game development and AI internally. He also has given talks at multiple schools about getting into game development and programming as a career. More recently, he released a game development book on C# and XNA, which had 2,000 downloads in the first week. He also runs Learn Build Play, a small private school dedicated to teaching game development and design mostly with C# and Unity 3D.

He can be contacted at `Dan.Sagmiller@LearnBuildPlay.com`.

About the Reviewers

Davide Aversa graduated in Computer Science with a Master's degree in Artificial Intelligence and Robotics. Currently, he is a PhD student at La Sapienza University of Rome, where he works on game AI, character behavior, and computational creativity.

Adam Boyce is a software developer and independent game developer who specializes in C# scripting, game design, and AI development. His experience includes application support, software development, and data architecture with various Canadian corporations. This is his first technical review for Packt Publishing. You can read his development blog at www.gameovertures.ca and follow him on Twitter at @AdamBoyce4.

> I'd like to thank my wife, Gail, for her support through this process and her patience with my late-night code review sessions.

Jesse Lu has been a Unity 3D programmer for 5 years. In these years, he developed some games with Unity 3D, for example, 《王途霸业》, 《凡人修仙》, 《临兵斗者三国志》, and so on.

Brent Owens is a full stack software engineer with more than 10 years of professional experience. His drive to help the open source community has led him to contribute to several open source projects, and become a core developer of the Java game engine, jMonkeyEngine. During his career, he worked on numerous game development tutorials and game projects and created the RTS game, *Attack of the Gelatinous Blob*.

He has also contributed to the book, *jMonkeyEngine 3.0 Beginner's Guide*, *Packt Publishing*.

I would like to thank Hilary for always supporting my endeavors and long hours contributing to game development.

Angelo Tadres is a Chilean software engineer with more than 7 years of professional experience. Hailing from Santiago, Chile, he began his career in R&D for video games meant to assist the blind and visually impaired with their orientation and mobility skills. After a quick pass through the telecommunications industry — working in value-added services and mobile applications — he received the opportunity to join the Santiago studio of DeNA, one of the world's largest mobile video game companies. In 2013, Angelo was asked to move to Vancouver, Canada, as a lead software engineer, where he helped to build the fledgling Canadian studio to a team of 90, and in particular, championed Unity 3D, paving the way for other teams' adoption and use of this technology. He's known for getting things done, shooting first and asking questions later. When he is not coding and pushing to GitHub, you'll find him playing table tennis or running along the sea wall. Visit his website at http://angelotadres.com.

Francisco Ureña has a degree in Philosophy and is a backend programmer in Realcom Code, for both mobile applications and servers. He is also an indie game developer in a small independent studio in Seville called Plasma Toy Studios, where he is currently developing the game Anarchy.

www.PacktPub.com

Support files, eBooks, discount offers, and more

For support files and downloads related to your book, please visit www.PacktPub.com.

Did you know that Packt offers eBook versions of every book published, with PDF and ePub files available? You can upgrade to the eBook version at www.PacktPub.com and as a print book customer, you are entitled to a discount on the eBook copy. Get in touch with us at service@packtpub.com for more details.

At www.PacktPub.com, you can also read a collection of free technical articles, sign up for a range of free newsletters and receive exclusive discounts and offers on Packt books and eBooks.

https://www2.packtpub.com/books/subscription/packtlib

Do you need instant solutions to your IT questions? PacktLib is Packt's online digital book library. Here, you can search, access, and read Packt's entire library of books.

Why subscribe?

- Fully searchable across every book published by Packt
- Copy and paste, print, and bookmark content
- On demand and accessible via a web browser

Free access for Packt account holders

If you have an account with Packt at www.PacktPub.com, you can use this to access PacktLib today and view 9 entirely free books. Simply use your login credentials for immediate access.

Table of Contents

Preface

Welcome to *Unity AI Programming Essentials*. This book will guide you through all the skills necessary to put realistic game AI into your Unity games. We won't be spending much time discussing AI theory or how to implement popular AI algorithms from scratch. Instead, we will take the more efficient approach of using third-party Unity AI plugins to set up AI for your games easily. We will cover all the essential game AI skills, such as pathfinding to have your characters navigate a game scene, behavior trees to let them "think", and sensors so that they can react to their environment. We'll also cover more specialized tasks such as setting up crowds and cars for driving and integrating animation. By the end of the book, you should know all the basic skills you need to create game AI with Unity.

What this book covers

Chapter 1, Pathfinding, covers how to set up basic pathfinding so that game characters can navigate a game scene realistically.

Chapter 2, Patrolling, extends our pathfinding to have characters patrol routes in a scene.

Chapter 3, Behavior Trees, explains behavior trees and how they are used to give AI characters the ability to make decisions.

Chapter 4, Crowd Chaos, focuses on creating a wander behavior that can be used to create ambient crowds.

Chapter 5, Crowd Control, demonstrates using specialized crowd plugins how to generate groups of AI characters.

Chapter 6, Sensors and Activities, shows how to set up sensors and have AI characters change their activity based on what they sense in the environment.

Chapter 7, Adaptation, shows how to have AI characters react and adapt to different events in the game.

Chapter 8, Attacking, discusses different techniques to have an enemy AI attack the player.

Chapter 9, Driving, shows how to set up driving AI that uses a car's physics to generate realistic driving behavior.

Chapter 10, Animation and AI, discusses how to integrate character animation with AI using both Unity's legacy and Mecanim animation systems.

Chapter 11, Advanced NavMesh Generation, discusses more advanced options for setting up navigation meshes to handle mesh creation for different geometries and multiple NavMeshs in a scene.

What you need for this book

This book uses Unity 4 with a standard license. Additionally, it uses RAIN, a Unity AI plugin that is available for free from `http://rivaltheory.com/rain/`. Additional plugins are used such as React AI and AI plugins for crowds and driving that can be purchased from the Asset Store, for which details are provided in the appropriate chapters.

Who this book is for

This book is aimed at developers who know the basics of game development with Unity and want to learn how to add AI to their games. You do not need any previous AI knowledge; this book will explain all the essential AI concepts and show you how to add and use them in your games.

Conventions

In this book, you will find a number of styles of text that distinguish between different kinds of information. Here are some examples of these styles, and an explanation of their meaning.

Code words in text, database table names, folder names, filenames, file extensions, pathnames, dummy URLs, user input, and Twitter handles are shown as follows: "We find all the `NavigationTargetRig` objects and store them in the `coverPoints` array."

A block of code is set as follows:

```
public override void Start(AI ai)
{
```

```
    base.Start(ai);

    ai.WorkingMemory.SetItem("donePatrolling", true);
}
```

New terms and **important words** are shown in bold. Words that you see on the screen, in menus or dialog boxes for example, appear in the text like this: "In the AI game object/component that was added, from the **Mind** tab, set **Behavior Tree Asset** to **RandomWalk**."

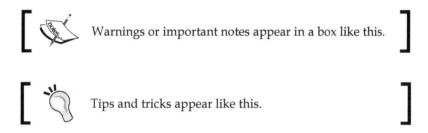

Warnings or important notes appear in a box like this.

Tips and tricks appear like this.

Reader feedback

Feedback from our readers is always welcome. Let us know what you think about this book—what you liked or disliked. Reader feedback is important for us as it helps us develop titles that you will really get the most out of.

To send us general feedback, simply e-mail feedback@packtpub.com, and mention the book's title in the subject of your message.

If there is a topic that you have expertise in and you are interested in either writing or contributing to a book, see our author guide at www.packtpub.com/authors.

Customer support

Now that you are the proud owner of a Packt book, we have a number of things to help you to get the most from your purchase.

Downloading the example code

You can download the example code files from your account at http://www.packtpub.com for all the Packt Publishing books you have purchased. If you purchased this book elsewhere, you can visit http://www.packtpub.com/support and register to have the files e-mailed directly to you.

Downloading the color images of this book

We also provide you with a PDF file that has color images of the screenshots/diagrams used in this book. The color images will help you better understand the changes in the output. You can download this file from: `https://www.packtpub.com/sites/default/files/downloads/3556OT_ColoredImages.pdf`.

Errata

Although we have taken every care to ensure the accuracy of our content, mistakes do happen. If you find a mistake in one of our books—maybe a mistake in the text or the code—we would be grateful if you could report this to us. By doing so, you can save other readers from frustration and help us improve subsequent versions of this book. If you find any errata, please report them by visiting `http://www.packtpub.com/submit-errata`, selecting your book, clicking on the **Errata Submission Form** link, and entering the details of your errata. Once your errata are verified, your submission will be accepted and the errata will be uploaded to our website or added to any list of existing errata under the Errata section of that title.

To view the previously submitted errata, go to `https://www.packtpub.com/books/content/support` and enter the name of the book in the search field. The required information will appear under the **Errata** section.

Piracy

Piracy of copyrighted material on the Internet is an ongoing problem across all media. At Packt, we take the protection of our copyright and licenses very seriously. If you come across any illegal copies of our works in any form on the Internet, please provide us with the location address or website name immediately so that we can pursue a remedy.

Please contact us at `copyright@packtpub.com` with a link to the suspected pirated material.

We appreciate your help in protecting our authors and our ability to bring you valuable content.

Questions

If you have a problem with any aspect of this book, you can contact us at `questions@packtpub.com`, and we will do our best to address the problem.

1
Pathfinding

Probably the most useful game AI is pathfinding. Pathfinding is all about making your way from one point to another while navigating around obstacles. Unity excels at linking the worlds of designers and programmers. AI is no different, and we'll see how to make simple pathfinding AIs without ever touching the code. Pathfinding is probably the most common AI game task, and there are many Unity plugins for it. We will be looking at three different ones.

In this chapter, you will learn:

- Working with pathfinding
- Applying pathfinding in Quick Path, React, and RAIN AI packages
- Behavior trees
- Applying characters to Character Controller
- Unity's NavMesh

An overview

Pathfinding is a way to get an object from point A to point B. Assuming that there are no obstacles, the object can just be moved in the direction of the target. But the AI part of it is all about navigating the obstacles.

A poor AI might try walking a **Non-Player Character** (**NPC**) directly to the target. Then, if it is blocked, it randomly tries to go to the right or left to look for a space that might help. The character can get caught in different areas and become permanently stuck.

A better AI will walk an NPC in an intelligent way to a target, and will never get stuck in different areas. To compute a good path for the NPC to walk, the AI system will use a graph that represents the game level, and a graph search algorithm is used to find the path. The industry-standard algorithm for pathfinding is **A* (A Star)**, a quick graph search algorithm that uses a cost function between nodes — in pathfinding usually the distance — and the algorithm tries to minimize the overall cost (distance) of the path. If you want to learn to code your own pathfinding AI, try A* because it is simple to implement and has a lot of simple improvements that you can apply for your game's needs.

The AIs we are about to discuss will take care of the pathfinding algorithms for you, and ultimately reduce the time it takes to breathe AI life into your game. Now let's look at Quick Path AI.

Quick Path AI

Alekhine Games' Quick Path is a \$10 AI that you can pick up from the Unity Asset Store. Although the next two AIs have more features, this AI is added because of its blocky nature. This block approach creates a grid-based path and is used with many types of games, but this AI works especially well with the excitement in the voxel game genre; it is suited for cubed topography.

To start with, perform the following steps:

1. Create a new 3D scene and import the Quick Path AI from the Asset Store.

2. Next, set up some cubes, planes, or other objects as your terrain, and then place all of these game objects into an empty game object. Name this game object `Terrain`.

3. Next, on the **Inspector** panel, add a component, **QuickPath | Grid**. Immediately, you should see a series of blue lines that show up on the cubes. These indicate all the points where a character can move in the AI.

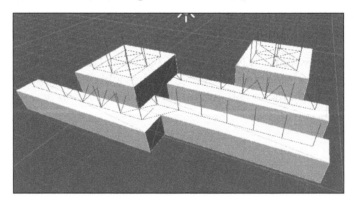

4. Now, we need a character to move around the scene. Create a sphere, or any object, and name it NPC.

5. Then, we'll add a Component, **QuickPath | AI | Follow Mouse Object**.

6. Now, when you run the scene, assuming it is lit up and has the camera pointing where you want it to, you'll see NPC on Terrain.

7. Click somewhere on the Terrain object, and watch the NPC object move to that point.

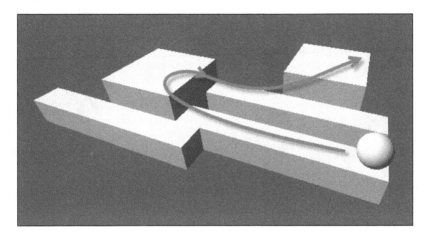

8. Although we might say that the pathfinding in this is clearly working, we should also add an obstacle to the scene: something that shouldn't be stepped on. To do this, add another cube somewhere. Go to the **Inspector** panel for the obstacle and tag it with **Obstacle** by selecting that tag from the drop-down, or if it is not an option select **Add Tag...** and add Obstacle to the tag list.

9. Next, in the Terrain game object, in the **Grid** component, expand **Disallowed Tags**, increase the size to 1 and enter **Obstacle** for the new element.

10. Next, click on the **Bake** button at the top of the **Grid** component. Now you will see that the grid markers skipped the cube as an option. If you want to test more, click somewhere else on the `Terrain` object and watch the `NPC` object move to the clicked point avoiding the obstacle.

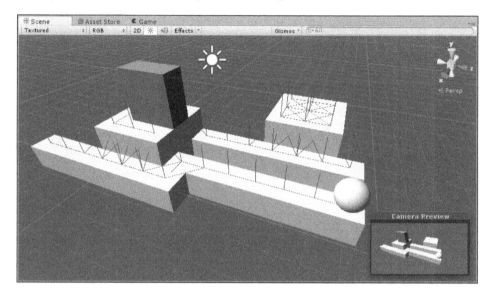

Now, we've seen how to set up pathfinding with Quick Path, so let's look at another way to set up pathfinding with React AI.

React AI

Different Methods' React, a $45 AI, introduces a behavior tree and the use of a navigation mesh, or NavMesh. A **NavMesh** is a series of interconnected polygons forming a complex area used for travel. It creates a simplified graph of the level that is inputted into the pathfinding system. This simplified graph that it creates is smoother and tends to have characters that travel better than a grid-based graph. A behavior tree is a parent-child structure used for making decisions in many AIs. We will look at behavior trees and navigation meshes in more detail in the later chapters. NavMesh is a basic feature available in Unity, but the behavior tree is not. Unlike the other two AIs shown, this AI requires a bit more coding to get started, but not much.

To begin with, you'll need a new scene, as well as to import React AI from the Asset Store. Perform the following steps:

1. Add a plane or another ground type. Then add several obstacle objects, such as cubes. Make sure that each of the objects we just created are marked static at the top of the Inspector, or the NavMesh won't identify them later on. The scene should look like this:

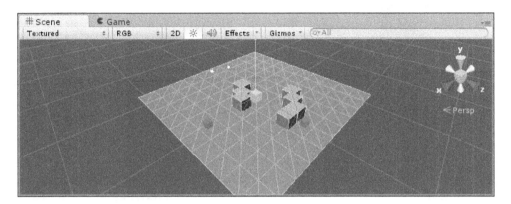

2. Next, find the **Window** menu and select **Navigation**. At the bottom of the **Navigation** tab, click on the **Bake** command. You have now generated a simple navigation mesh for your characters to navigate. It will highlight the areas that NavMesh AIs can walk, as seen here:

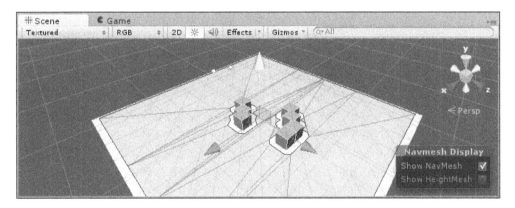

3. Let's add a player who can move around the world now. Add a capsule and name it `Player`. Fortunately, the demo contains a simple script for controlling a player who you can find (and add) by navigating to **Add Component | Scripts | Simple Player Control**. Now, this doesn't move the object around on its own; instead it drives a **Character Controller** object.

> **Character Controller** is a type of an object that you can inherit in your code classes that many AIs can operate. In this case, there is a basic Character Controller type to simply move a given object around.

4. When adding the component, just start typing `Character Controller` in the search box, and it will show you all the similar component names. Add **Character Controller**. Now, the player should be controllable. You will probably need to increase the speed to 1 to detect the player movement.

> Make sure that the game object, and any body parts, do not have collider components. Controllers detect colliders to determine whether or not they can move to a given place.

5. Next, we'll add an enemy in the same way, with **Capsule**. The enemy needs a component called **Nav Mesh Agent**, which is a component capable of using a NavMesh to move around, so add it. Now, the game object has the ability to walk around, but it has nowhere to go. To get it moving, we need to add the enemy AI agent.

6. Next, we get to the AI for the enemy agent. In React, a behavior tree is called a **Reactable**. To add a reactor, we start the **Project** explorer, in a folder of our choice, by navigating to **Create | Reactable**.

7. Once created, rename it to `EnemyMovement`. In the Inspector, it has a list of behaviors for it. We'll need to add a script, which can be found in the book's contents: `\Scripts\React AI\FollowThePlayer.cs`. Without going in-depth in the code, let me explain the following key points:

    ○   The C# file was copied from a sample script provided with React AI that made a character move away from a target.

    ○   It was rebuilt to make the player the target destination, and also to turn seeking on and off by using a button. It is not hard to adapt these scripts.

    ○   Unlike normal mono behaviors, you use a special `Go` method. The go method is called by React AI only if it is selected to be used.

    ○   In the `Start` method, we see it obtain the NavMeshAgent that we attached to the enemy in the Inspector panel.

    ○   In the `Go` method, we see it feeding the destination to the NavMeshAgent, and then checking to see whether it has already found a path. Once it does, it just goes.

      °   All uses of that agent are still following standard Unity calls to use NavMesh, and can be applied without using the AI, by placing this code in a traditional behavior `Update` method.

    This script needs to be added to the Inspector for the **EnemyMovement** asset, and also to the `Enemy` game object.

8. Once the script is attached to the enemy, the Inspector will reveal that it has a target. Drag the player from the **Hierarchy** panel into the player attribute on the **Inspector** panel.

9. Finally, we have the behavior tree to set up. In the **Project** panel, right-click on the **EnemyMovement** asset, and click on **Edit Reactable**. A behavior tree pops up an editor, which is how we train our AI.

For this chapter, we'll just give it a one track mind to follow the player. With **Root** selected, click on the **Action** button under **Leaf**, as shown in the following screenshot:

Since we only have one action in the behavior list, it selects it by default. What makes the behavior tree nice is that we can make decisions, or check whether the target is within X distance then try to follow, otherwise do something else–all from the designer. The next section on RAIN also uses a behavior tree, and most of the same basic types are used in both RAIN and React.

This took more steps than the previous AI, but there is also more going on. It is playable now.

Downloading the example code

You can download the example code files from your account at `http://www.packtpub.com` for all the Packt Publishing books you have purchased. If you purchased this book elsewhere, you can visit `http://www.packtpub.com/support` and register to have the files e-mailed directly to you.

RAIN AI

Rival Theory's RAIN AI is a very full-featured AI to use and it is free. It includes a behavior tree with similar functionality to React, but has more features built in. In fact, this one won't require any additional scripting to go from point A to point B.

To get this going, we'll need the following bases:

- A map to move around on
- A character to move around in the map
- A route (series of waypoints) for the character to follow
- A navigation mesh that knows what to avoid
- An AI to control the character
- A behavior tree to tell the AI what to do

To start with, you'll need to start a new Unity project, import Unity's Character Controller, and import the RAIN AI package.

 Don't get the RAIN AI package that is found in the Asset store. The current release (at the time of writing this book) can be found at the Rival Theory site, `rivaltheory.com/rain/`.

Perform the following steps:

1. To create our map, add a plane. Then, add a couple of objects to act as obstacles. It is best if they create a *U* or *V* shape to potentially trap the player:

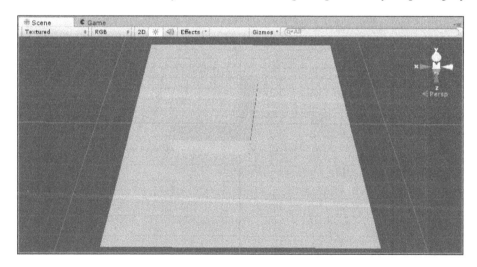

2. Next, drag the predefined character found in **Project | Standard Assets | Character Controllers | Sources | Prototype Character | "constructor"** into the scene. From the scene depicted in the preceding screenshot, I recommend placing him (the character) on the back left-hand side of the plane.

3. Next, we need a route. Although there is more than one waypoint system in RAIN, I found that the route will be the fastest for this demo. In the **RAIN** menu, click on **Create Waypoint Route**. Name it's game object GreenPath. We will need to call this later, so we want simple, easy names to remember.

4. In the **Inspector** panel for GreenPath, click on the **Add (Ctrl W)** button. This adds a waypoint. In fact, we need to add three. Place the first one on the inside of the V, the second on the tip of the V, and the last on the far edge of the plane, as shown in the following screenshot:

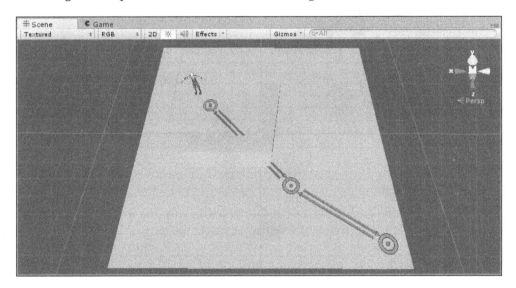

5. Just as in React AI and Unity NavMesh, we need a navigation mesh for this as well. We clearly defined the route, but as you can see, the path is blocked. In the RAIN menu, click on **Create Navigation Mesh**. Align and stretch it so that it surrounds the area where you want the paths to be determined.

The Inspector panel for the NavMesh has a property called **Ignored Tags**. Add **Player** to this list. (You might need to make sure that the player object actually has that tag selected as well.) Otherwise, the NavMesh will not generate where the player stands, and will prevent its ability to find a path. Then click on **Generate Navigation Mesh** at the bottom of the **Inspector** panel. The result should look like this:

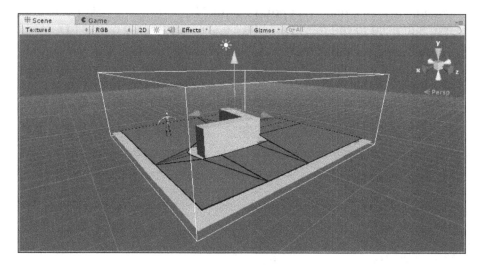

6. Next, we need to add an AI to control the character. Select the player object in the **Hierarchy** panel, and from the **RAIN** menu, click on **Create AI**.

7. Next, select the middle button of the character running in the AI **Inspector** panel, then click on the **Add Existing Animations** button at the bottom. This will add all the player's animations: idle, walk, jump, pose, and run. You can refer to the following screenshot:

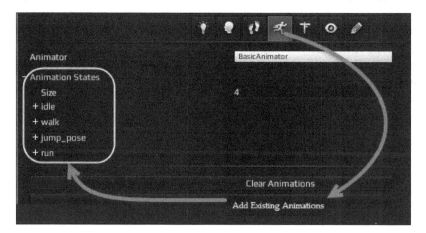

8. Next, we need to add a behavior tree. Behavior trees are a way to define decisions and actions for AI characters. We will discuss them in more detail in *Chapter 3, Behavior Trees*. For now, add one by clicking on the head/brain icon in the **Inspector** panel and then click on the **Open Behaviour Editor button**. On the right-hand side is a behavior tree drop-down selector, so click on it and choose **Create New Behaviour Tree**.

9. Name it **FollowGreenRoad**. It will already have one element, **SEQ** (**Sequence**), under the root **BT** (**behavior tree**) node. Sequence it means that it will run any child nodes in order. Right-click on the **SEQ** node and navigate to **Switch To | Parallel**, which means that it will run all its child nodes simultaneously.

10. Let's add the child nodes and then set them up. Right-click on the **PAR** node, then navigate to **Create | Actions | Animations**. Right-click on **PAR** again and navigate to **Create | Actions | Choose Patrol Waypoints**. Then right-click on the new **WAY** node and navigate to **Create | Actions | Move**.

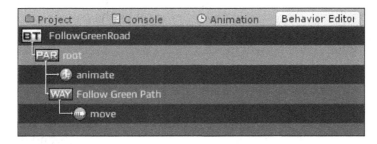

Because the decision is to run things in parallel, it will animate the character and follow the waypoints at the same time.

11. Click on the green **animate** node, and set its animation state to **walk**. It is case sensitive, but you can select which animation the character should use.

12. Next, select the **WAY** node. Here, you need to set **Waypoint Route** to use. This was the navigation route we created earlier with the three waypoints. We called it GreenPath.

13. For the loop type, we'll make it **One Way** so that the character only travels to the end and stops there. Also, change the name of the loop to **Follow Green Path**. This shows up next to the **WAY** node, and helps explain what is happening.

14. Finally, set the Move Target Variable to **NextWayPoint**. This is a variable that we are setting with the next waypoint in the path. When it is reached, the patrol route will set the variable to the next location in the path. We use this in the Move node.

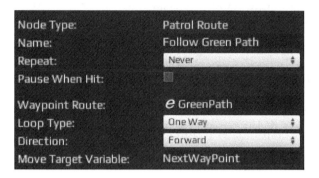

15. Select the **move** node, and in the properties, set the **Move Target** to **NextWayPoint**, the variable that is being set by the patrol route we just configured. And set the **Move Speed** to a number, such as 3. This is how fast the character will move.

16. Now that we have created the behavior tree, we need to set the Character AI to use it. Select the AI object under the player object in the Hierarchy panel. On the Mind icon, for the **Behavior Tree Asset**, set it to **FollowGreenRoad**. This can be found by navigating to **Project | AI | Behavior Trees**, or from the selector in the **Inspector** panel, choose the **Assets** tab, and it should be right on top.

The demo should be able to run now. The character will move around the block and walk to the last waypoint in the path.

Comparing AI solutions

Each AI has its own strengths and weaknesses, ranging from price to flexibility to designer friendliness. Also, each AI has more than one way to accomplish this chapter's task of moving a character from point A to point B. We selected paths that were faster and easier to start with, but keep in mind that each of them has plenty of flexibility. All three proved to work well as terrain/trees as well as simple planes and cubes.

Experiences of working with all three:

- Quick Path is a good choice for a beginner. It has the fewest steps to do to get going, and works easily. Quick Path is focused on just pathfinding and the others are larger AI systems that can be expanded to many more areas because of their use of behavior trees.

- RAIN has many features beyond pathfinding that we will discuss in future chapters. The learning curve for RAIN is higher than Quick Path and unlike other AI solutions, the source code is unavailable, but it is a good all-round solution for game AI. And while RAIN has the ability to be customized through user-defined scripts, the focus is on easy AI setup through the Unity GUI without needing to write scripts often.

- React includes a behavior, but requires more code to get it running, which is good if you are interested in coding more. You build all the actions it can use, and let the designers focus on the tree. RAIN can do this too, but with React, you are building the blocks from square one.

Overall, the best AI for you is the one best suited for your game and that you enjoy using. We will be looking at these three and other AI systems in detail throughout this book.

Summary

Our AI characters need to be able to move between different points in our scene in an intelligent way, and we looked at pathfinding AI systems that helped us do that. We tried three different ones: Quick Path, React, and RAIN. But our characters need to be able to do more than just walk from one point to a second one in our levels. In the next chapter, we will extend what we have learned about pathfinding here by seeing how to set up patrolling behaviors for our characters. This will be the start for having characters walk around a level in a realistic way.

2
Patrolling

Patrolling is a simple extension to pathfinding. Instead of just having a single target in mind, we might have two or more points. We might go back and forth between them, or travel in a never-ending loop.

In this chapter, you will learn about:

- How patrolling works
- Patrolling in Quick Path, React, and RAIN AI packages
- Getting to know more about behavior trees
- Creating patrols that go to different points in a level by not always following the same path

Patrolling is a way to get an object from point A to point B and then to point C, and so on. Pathfinding is still required to get from one waypoint to another, but here, we daisy-chain them into a larger, more meaningful path.

Quick Path AI

Quick Path is back again, with built-in capabilities to handle patrol. With its simple approach to AI, only a few straightforward steps are needed to get a scene finished. Here is a breakdown of these steps:

- Making the world ready for patrol
- Setting up the patrol script

We'll start by expanding on our world from *Chapter 1, Pathfinding* the quick path demo. Stretch out a couple of the blocks to make a larger surface area. Then, click on the terrain object (the parent of all the cubes forming the terrain), and in the **Inspector**, click on the **Bake** button. You can see what happens next in the following screenshot:

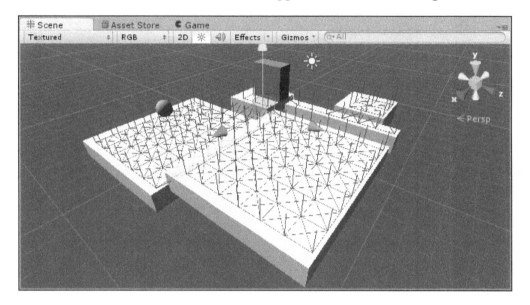

If the **Bake** function isn't covering all the areas, you'll need to check its grid dimensions. X remains the same in the world space, but Y is actually the Z axis. You might need to increase or decrease these numbers to cover everything in the scene:

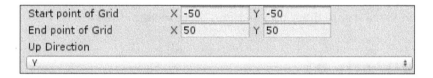

Quick Path converts the values of the Y or Z axis values internally. By default, it is set to Y as the *Up/Down* axis, but you can change this with the **Up Direction** parameter.

Now that we have a larger surface area to work with, we'll get the NPC object set up to patrol. If the object still has the following script, you will need to remove it, but then add the Quick Path patrol script. Then, the first thing to do in the **Inspector** panel for the patrol script is change the speed to 2, as its default of 10 was rather fast.

Next, set **Spill Distance** to 0.1. **Spill Distance** is how close you have to be to a waypoint before it picks the next waypoint as your target. If **Ping Pong** is checked, the NPC will stop at the end of its path and backtrack. If it is unchecked, at the end of its path, it will target the first position and start over.

Pathfinding Between Points is an option that helps it navigate around obstacles between waypoints. If your path is already clear, then you can keep this option off and save extra processing.

Finally, we have **Patrol Path**, which houses the waypoints for the NPC to travel on. Increase this to 3, and then set the waypoints. A trick to figure out the values is to move your NPC in the scene to the waypoint positions that you want and then copy its position to one of the waypoints. So, select three points for your NPC to travel on. You can refer to the following screenshot for the settings:

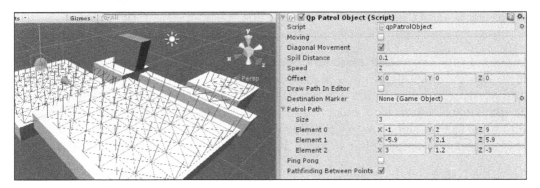

Now, your game is ready to run, with your NPC navigating a course that you just set up.

React AI

React AI doesn't come equipped with a patrol script, so we provided one. We'll start with this behavior tree script and look at how it works and how to use it. Here are the steps to reproduce it:

1. Create a patrol script.
2. Create a patrol AI.
3. Set up the NPC patrol.

To start with, we've provided a script for you to use. In it, I started with the last script for pathfinding, and then I extended it to use a similar configuration to the patrol path in Quick Path's patrol script. Here are a couple of key points about this script:

- It is based on the `FollowThePlayer` script from the previous chapter.
- You can find the code in the book's contents at `\Scripts\React AI\Patrol.cs`.

- It stores a public array of `Vector3`, so the **Inspector** UI can allow designers to set the waypoints.

- Instead of the target being a player, it is set to the next waypoint in the list. Once we are close enough, it selects the next waypoint. **Close Enough** is the float field that allows the inspector to find it.

- If there are no waypoints left to select, it starts over at the first waypoint.

However, now we need to create the user endpoint. Right-click on a folder in the **Project** tab and choose **Create | Reactable**. Name the reactable `PatrolAI`. In its **Inspector** UI, add the patrol script as one of the behaviors. Next, right-click on the **PatrolAI** asset and select **Edit Reactable**.

In the reactable, right-click on the root element and select **AddBranch | Sequence**. A sequence repeats all the steps in an order. Under the **Sequence** option, right-click and navigate to **Add | Leaf | Action**. Assuming that you only added the patrol script to its behaviors, it should automatically select **Patrol.Go** as its action. You can add notes to each step to help write a better story of what the AI is doing. When it is this simple, it does not matter so much, but many AIs will become more complex.

Next, the NPC needs to be set up to use this new patrol AI. Find the NPC in the previous chapter's React AI project. You'll need to remove the following AI that was on the NPC before, or create a new NPC. If you create a new NPC, do not forget to add the NavMesh agent so that it can navigate.

Add two components to the NPC: **Reactor** and **Patrol**. In the **Reactor** component, you will need to set the **Reactable** value to the **Patrol AI** asset that we created earlier. Then, in the patrol script, add some waypoints. Like we did for the Quick Path patrol script, we need to set the **Vector** locations for each of the waypoints.

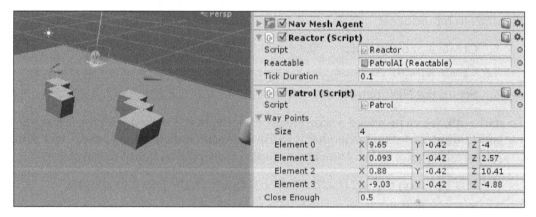

A tip to get exact numbers is to just move the NPC to the waypoint positions you want and then copy the position of the NPC to one of the waypoints.

Now your game should have a character who patrols from point to point.

RAIN AI

RAIN has this section put together pretty well. In reality, we only have one small section to change from the pathfinding demo, especially because the pathfinding demo had actually turned off the patrol feature.

Start with the project for RAIN AI from *Chapter 1, Pathfinding*. From the menu, navigate to **RAIN | Behavior Tree Editor**. From the editor, select **FollowGreenRoad**. Under **Sequence** is a patrol route node called **waypointpatrol**; select it. Finally, we have a property called **Loop Type**. Presently, it is on **One Way**, which stops at the last waypoint. You can switch it to **Ping Pong** or **Loop**, as shown in the following screenshot:

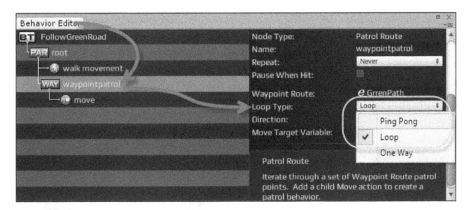

Ping Pong bounces you back and forth on the path, while **Loop** connects the last waypoint to the first to start over.

This works when creating a typical patrolling behavior, where a character loops along a path. However, what if we want to have a character patrol an area by walking around back and forth to different points without always following the same route? In RAIN AI, we can do this by using a waypoint network instead of a waypoint graph and updating our behavior tree to randomly pick different points in the level to go to.

To illustrate this, create a new scene, and like in our current patrol example, add a character and some blocks and create a navigation mesh. Separate the blocks a bit so that we can add different paths in between them. You can refer to the next screenshot to view this setup:

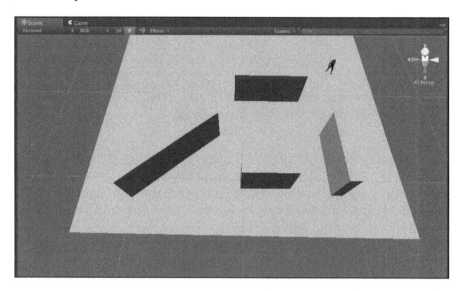

In this demo, we will have the character walk to different points outside the walls, but when patrolling, the character won't go in a circle outside the walls; instead, it will always walk through the middle. To do this, we will need a waypoint network similar to the one shown in the following screenshot:

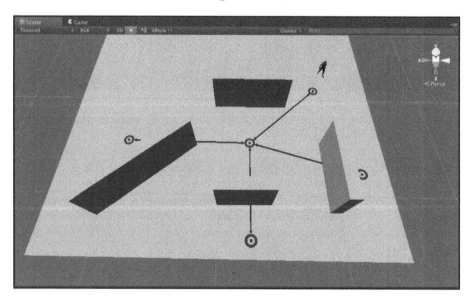

To add a waypoint, navigate to **RAIN | Create Waypoint Network**. Then, set up the network similar to how you set up a waypoint route, by creating different points. However, unlike a waypoint route, with a waypoint network you can also connect different points. To connect two waypoints, select them by pressing *Ctrl + Shift* and left-clicking the mouse and then click on **Connect** in the **RAIN Waypoint Network** component menu. Connect the points in a *plus sign* shape as illustrated in the previous screenshot. With this network, to walk from the side of one wall to another, the character will always need to walk through the middle of the scene.

The network waypoint describes how a character should walk to different spots on a level, but it actually doesn't contain the different points we can tell the AI character to go to. If we want to tell our character to go to a specific location, we need what RAIN calls a navigation target. A navigation target is just an object that contains a point in the scene that we can use with the rest of the AI system. You can create navigation targets by navigating to **RAIN | Create Navigation Target** and place them like you would place a waypoint. Create three navigation targets and place them on the side of three walls. We will follow a convention used in other RAIN examples and name the navigation targets Location1, Location2, and Location3, as shown in the following screenshot:

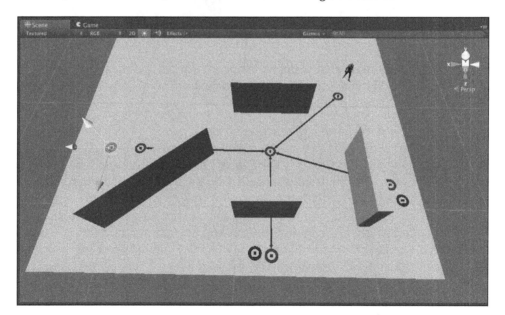

The Inspector panel should look like the following screenshot:

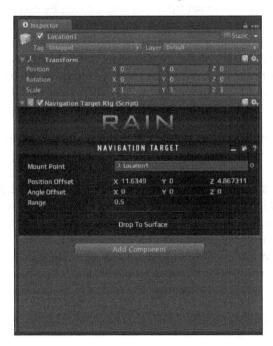

This is all of the scene setup that we need to specify routes and locations for the character to walk. However, we will need to customize the behavior tree to randomly choose different points to patrol to.

Create a new behavior tree for our character and call it `Patrol`. Open the behavior tree editor, and below the new root node, create a **Random** node by right-clicking on the root and navigating to **Create | Decisions | Random**. This creates a node that randomly selects one of its children to execute. Don't worry too much about how the different nodes work in the RAIN behavior tree for now; we will go into more detail about them in the next chapter. For now, create three expression nodes as children of the **Random** node by right-clicking on **Random** and navigating to **Create | Actions | Expression**. An expression node allows us to execute a single statement, which is called an expression in RAIN. Rename the expression nodes Choose Location 1, Choose Location 2, Choose Location 3. Then, in the expression field for the nodes, set the first to `location = navigationtarget(Location1)`, and do the same for the other location expression nodes, using numbers 2 and 3. These expression nodes create a variable location that is a randomly determined navigation target that we can use as a target to walk to. The setup should look like this:

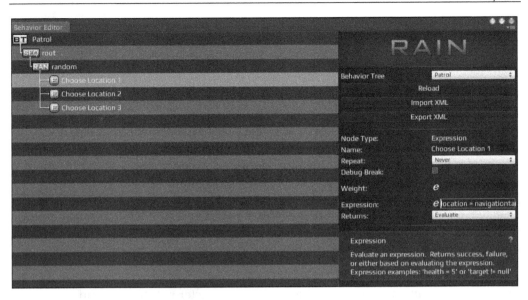

All that is left is to add nodes to walk to the target. Right-click on the root node and navigate to **Create | Decisions | Waypoint Path** (not waypoint patrol like last time). In the waypoint path node, set the **Waypoint Network** field to PatrolNetwork (with quotes) to tell it which network to use. Set the **Path Target** field to location (without quotes), which is the variable we stored our random target to walk to. Finally, set up the rest of the tree as shown earlier, with an animation node and a child Move node. The final setup should look as shown in the following screenshot:

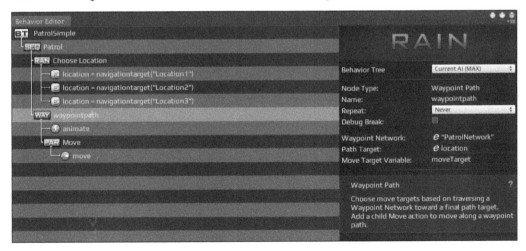

If you run the project now, the character will randomly patrol the area of the level by randomly walking from one navigation target location to the next and always walking through the middle of the level.

Summary

We were able to get patrolling operational in all three AIs. Each AI had its own approach.

For patrol as well as pathfinding, Quick Path had very few steps. If your need is mostly pathfinding, it does exactly what it claims to do easily. As for React, it does not have patrol out of the box, as we saw in the last chapter. However, it was not difficult to create a script that operates inside its behavior tree AI editor. This is a powerful system that you can use to allow designers to easily access and apply your awesome scripts, but you have to be comfortable programming to build the pieces for it. For RAIN, which made this about as easy as a big red button. With one setting changed, we changed the pathfinding AI into a patrolling AI. RAIN comes equipped with a huge variety of prebuilt character controlling; we looked at how to use a different waypoint system, a waypoint network, to give variety to our character when patrolling.

This concludes our chapters on setting up basic character pathfinding and movement. In later chapters, we will look in more detail at different aspects of this, such as animation and creating navigation meshes. In the next chapter, we will look at customizing our characters by investigating behavior trees in more detail. We will also learn to create more advanced setups using behavior trees.

3
Behavior Trees

When creating AI for game characters, we want them to appear to behave in realistic ways. This is done by defining different behaviors that a character can do, such as walking, patrolling, attacking, or searching for something, as well as how the character reacts to different items or events in the game environment. In addition to defining a character's behaviors, we need to define when the different behaviors occur. For example, instead of just following a path, we might want the character to change behaviors at different times. This chapter will look at the most popular way to define behaviors and when they occur: behavior trees. We have already looked at behavior trees in the previous chapters, but here, we will go into more detail.

In this chapter, we will learn about:

- How behavior trees work
- Implementing complex behavior trees
- RAIN's behavior trees and the different options that we have to configure them
- Setting up more advanced behavior trees with a character that has multiple objectives

An overview of behavior trees

For game AI, we need to define logic for the different AI entity characters in the game, that is, how they will act and react to different things in the game environment. The traditional and simpler way to do this is to use **Finite State Machines** (**FSMs**). In this approach, each character can be in a distinct state, and an FSM is a graph that defines states (nodes) and their transitions (edges). A simple example would be an enemy entity with two states, patrol and attack. The FSM will start in a patrol state, and when it gets close to a player, it transitions to an attack state. FSMs work for very simple state setups such as this, but they don't scale well, as the states and transitions have to be manually configured, usually through code. What if instead of the two states, our enemy character was more realistic and had 10 or even 100 different states, with many transitions between each? This becomes very difficult to manage and implement.

The popular alternative to FSMs is behavior trees. Behavior trees are a different way to define logic for characters that scale easily to having many states. Instead of defining states and transitions, behavior trees focus on defining behaviors, also called tasks, for characters. Each behavior is a node in the tree and can consist of different sub-behaviors; so, instead of a general graph, a tree is created of different behaviors, where each behavior is a node on the graph.

At every update for the character, the behavior tree is traversed, starting at the root node and searching down the tree. The different behavior nodes execute and return if the task is running, or has completed successfully or failed. If the node is in a running state, it is updated. Behavior trees are built by creating and configuring different behavior nodes.

We will focus on RAIN's behavior tree system in this chapter. We can use a different behavior tree system or create one from scratch; the basic logic is the same for all implementations. When using a behavior tree system, the most important thing to know are the different node types that we can use; so, let's look at RAIN's different behavior nodes.

RAIN node types

For the RAIN implementation of behavior trees, the behavior nodes are split into two categories: decisions and actions. Actions tell the AI system to actually do something; it is where the actual *work* of the AI is done. The most common action is the one we saw in the previous chapters, **move**, which tells the AI system to move a character. Besides move, here is a list of the current actions RAIN supports:

- **The Choose patrol path and Choose path waypoints**: These nodes help to move the AI through a network of waypoints.

- **Detect**: This finds other AI entities and areas marked in a scene. This node will be covered in *Chapter 6, Sensors and Activities*.

- **The Evaluate expression**: This node evaluates some logic, using RAIN's custom logic system. We will be discussing this node more in this chapter.

- **Animate and Mechanism**: These animation nodes manage different animations playing on the entity. We'll look at this node type more in *Chapter 10, Animation and AI*.

- **Play audio**: Plays an audio sound for the entity.

- **Wait for timer**: A timer that will pause for a given number of seconds.

- **Yield**: This node stops executing the behavior tree in the frame. This is useful for spreading expensive AI computation over several frames.

- **Custom action**: This is used to create an action that can't be defined with the other nodes.

> Custom actions and decisions nodes are very useful to define AI behaviors that are unavailable with the default node types. We will look at an example of a custom action later in this chapter. Although creating custom nodes is more work, don't hesitate to use one if needed; part of making good AI is customizing things specific for your game.

Decision nodes, as the name suggests, are used to decide how we traverse the tree. Actions are the final things the AI does, and decisions are used to determine which child nodes should be run:

- **Sequential**: This is the most straightforward decision node; it updates its children in an order until one of them fails.

- **Priority**: This is an action node that lets you set a priority, both when it's running and before it starts. A priority node will choose a child to run based on the different priorities of its children.

- **Selector**: This node keeps running through child nodes until one of them returns `true`.

- **Parallel**: This states to have its children nodes run at the same time. This is a common and useful node, and for cases such as a character walking to a goal and moving and animating the walk cycle, the entity needs to have a move and animate decision node running at the same time.

- **Iterator**: This is a *repeat* node; it lets you specify that you want its children updated, not just once in an update, but a specified number of times.

- **Constraint**: This node lets us define a logical expression, a statement that returns true or false, to control the tree flow.

- **Custom decision**: Like a custom action, this lets you define a decision node specific to your game.

The behavior tree demo

Now that we know about the different nodes we can use, we'll create a demo that shows how to use the action and decision nodes. The demo will show how to have a character perform multiple tasks. We will have an entity, an enemy spaceship, patrolling an area, but only for a given amount of time; then, the ship will return to its home base. The steps for this example might seem overly complicated and we could do a similar AI ourselves without behavior trees with a simple script by hardcoding the different states. However, remember that behavior trees are easily extendible and scalable. With this demo, instead of two behaviors, we could take time to create a more complex character, going up to about 30 behaviors easily, but extending a script to do that would be pretty complicated and hard to maintain.

The start of this is similar to the pathfinding and patrol RAIN demos, except we will use a spaceship model instead of a walking character. You'll need to create a simple scene with a ship model (the examples have a `ship.blend` model you can use) and an object for the home base. The initial setup should look something like this:

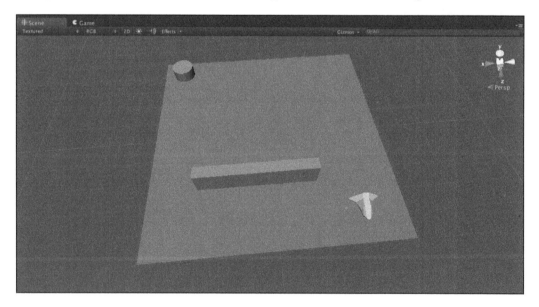

Then, add RAIN to the scene, create a waypoint route to patrol the block, create a navigation mesh, and add an AI to the ship. Remember that the ship model should not interfere with the navigation mesh creation; you can set it to a different layer, such as **Ignore Raycast**, and then in RAIN's navigation mesh menu, deselect this layer from the **Included Layers** dropdown:

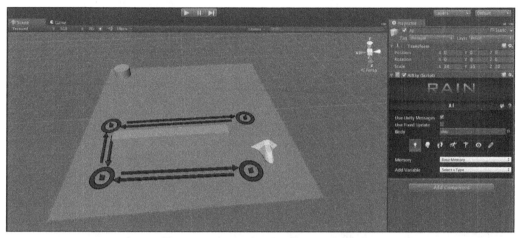

The scene after performing the given steps

In the AI for the ship, there is no behavior tree yet, so click on the **Mind** button in the RAIN menu (the little head icon) and then click on **Open Behavior Editor** and create a new behavior tree called `ship`:

Just like with the pathfinding demos, first we need to set up the behavior tree to have a basic waypoint route follow system. Under the root node in the behavior tree, we need to create a **waypointpatrol** node and a **move** node, with the **waypointpatrol** node set to use our waypoint route and setting its move variable to the **move** node. Do this by right-clicking on the root node and navigating to **Create | Actions | Choose Patrol Waypoints**. Then, right-click on the new **waypointpatrol** node and navigate to **Create | Actions | Move**. Then, set the **waypointpatrol** waypoint to **Patrol Route** (with quotes), the **Move Target Variable** field to move the target, and the **Repeat** type to **Forever**. The behavior tree should look like the following:

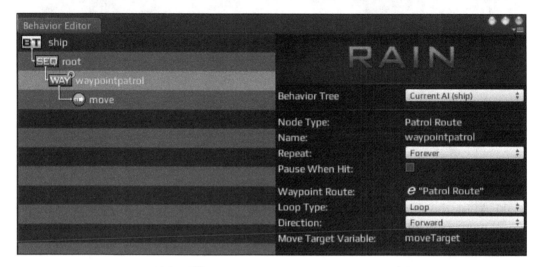

We'll speed up the ship movement, so select the **move** node and set the **Move Speed** value to 5.

When we run the demo now, the ship will patrol around the block, similar to our pathfinding demos. To extend this, we'll add an additional functionality of moving to a home base after a given number of seconds. However, two things need to be added to the scene before we make additions to the behavior tree. First, we need to create a navigation point for the home base so that the RAIN AI system can know where it is. In Unity, navigate to **RAIN | Create Navigation Target**. Rename both the GameObject and the target name in the RAIN menu for it to **gameBase**, and place it under our cylinder that visualizes our game base. This creates a new point RAIN can navigate to:

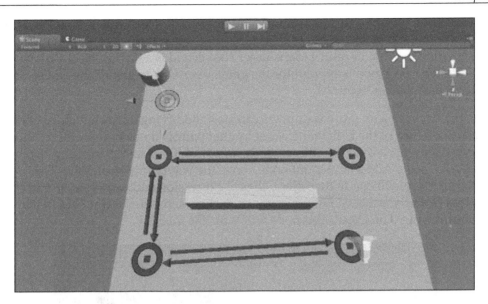

For our character logic, as we said we will have the entity patrol for a given number of seconds, then return to the home base. We'll use a Boolean variable to track whether the patrolling is done, but instead of just storing the variable in a script, we will have RAIN's memory system to store it. The memory for a character is what it *remembers* or *knows*. It is a way to store values that will be accessible to the other AI systems on a character. The possible values for memory are basic primitive variables such as bool, int, float, or vector, for example, Vector2, Vector3, Vector4, or a GameObject. We'll use two memory variables for this demo. Select the AI component of the ship and click on the **Memory** icon, which looks like a little light bulb, which you can see in the following screenshot:

Then, add two variables for the memory. The first is a Boolean called **donePatrolling**, which will initially be `false` but will become `true` when the 5-second timer runs out, signaling the ship to return to the base. The second is a GameObject variable that will store the navigation waypoint for the game base. Create **gameBase** and set it to the game base GameObject.

Now that we have a memory set up, we can start modifying our behavior tree. We already have part of the behavior tree set up that patrols the waypoint route. So, as a next step, we will only let the ship continue to patrol if our **donePatrolling** Boolean variable is `false`. Add a constraint node above the **waypointpatrol** node. The recall constraint is the node that uses a logical expression and can evaluate success or failure. Add the `donePatrolling == false` line to the constraint field in the **Constraint** node. The **Constraint** node will look like this:

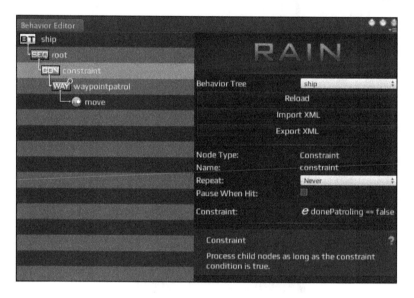

The little **e** symbol in the **Constraint** field means that it can take an expression, a one-line statement. This is done for simple checks and saves us from writing the code for a custom action node. Besides the basic Boolean test in this example, many other simple expressions can be created, for example, if we had an integer for an enemy's ammo amount, it can do a check to see how much ammo the character has, and if it is empty, it can stop attacking and instead go get more ammo. We can also have a check on an entity's health or HP, and if it's too low, a character can run away instead of fighting with the player. However, let's get back to our demo.

If we run the demo now, the ship will behave the same as before, but if we go into the memory for the character and change **donePatrolling** to true, the ship will do nothing when we start the demo:

The check in the preceding screenshot shows the **Constraint** node in action; however, go ahead and change the value of **donePatrolling** back to false.

Our additional logic for the ship's behavior tree is to return home after 5 seconds of patrolling. While the ship is patrolling, we want a timer running to 5 seconds. When the timer is complete, the **donePatrolling** variable will be set to `false`, stopping the patrol and the ship will start to move back to the **gameBase** navigation point. The first step for this is to right-click on the root node and navigate to **Switch To | Parallel**. Then, create a new sequencer node and add it to the root. The tree should look like this:

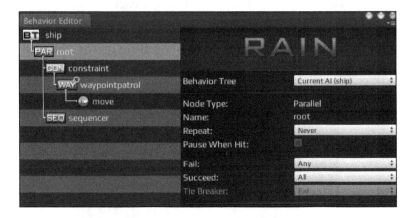

With the parallel node at every update, both of its children will be updated, allowing us to continue patrolling while we have a timer running. We want two things to happen if **donePatrolling** is `false`: the ship should continue to patrol and the timer should start to run. RAIN supports copying and pasting of nodes, so right-click on the **Constraint** node and select **Copy**, then right-click on the **sequencer** node and click on **Paste**. The node will be copied with its children, so delete the newly copied **waypointpatrol** and the **move** node. Then, add a **timer** action node below the second **Constraint** node, and set the time to 5 seconds. Now, the screen should look like this:

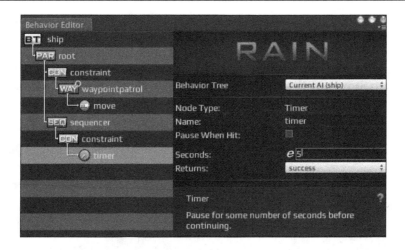

After the **timer** node, we need a node that will set the **donePatrolling** variable to
`true`. We can do this using an **expression** node and using its **Expression** value to
set **donePatrolling** to `true`. We use as shown in the next screenshot:

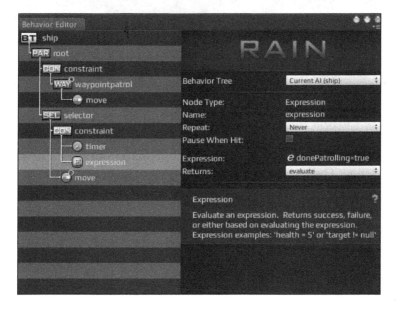

However, the ability to customize AI nodes is important, so instead of using an **expression** node again, we will use a **Custom Action** node. To create a **Custom Action** node, right-click on the lower **Constraint** node and navigate to **Create | Actions | Custom Action**. Change the name of the node (via the name field in the node editor) to **StopPatrolling**. For the **Class** value, choose **Create Custom Action**. The following screenshot will guide you through:

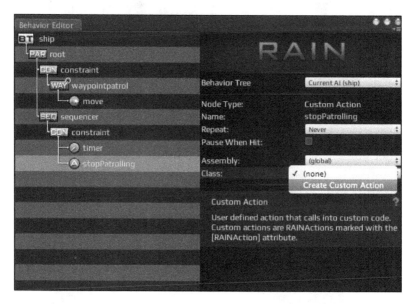

Set the name of **Custom Action Name** to **StopPatrolling** and leave the script type to **C Sharp**. Then, close the behavior tree editor and open the StopPatrolling.cs script from **Assets | AI | Actions**. The script contains an outline for an action that the user can define. The code is as follows:

```
using UnityEngine;
using System.Collections;
using System.Collections.Generic;
using RAIN.Core;
using RAIN.Action;

[RAINAction]
```

```
public class StopPatrolling : RAINAction
{
    public StopPatrolling()
    {
        actionName = "StopPatrolling";
    }

    public override void Start(AI ai)
    {
        base.Start(ai);
    }

    public override ActionResult Execute(AI ai)
    {
        return ActionResult.SUCCESS;
    }

    public override void Stop(AI ai)
    {
        base.Stop(ai);
    }
}
```

This contains the three basic methods you would expect to see in an action: one to call when the action is started, another when it is stopped, and an `Execute` method that is called when running the action that returns the state of the action node: success, failure, or running. With this outline, you can create all kinds of custom actions, but for now, all you need to do is set the `donePatrolling` variable in the memory to `true`. Change the `Start` method to the following:

```
public override void Start(AI ai)
{
    base.Start(ai);

    ai.WorkingMemory.SetItem("donePatrolling", true);
}
```

This code does what we need, setting the `donePatrolling` variable to `true`. The AI object in this code, just called `ai`, is the AI for the character. It contains access to various AI classes, such as the AI's mind and senses. Here, we access `WorkingMemory` and can get the different memory items as well as set values for them. That is all the action needs to do so that `ActionResult` can leave returning success.

If we run the project now, we should see the ship patrol for 5 seconds, but instead of moving back to the game base, the ship just stops. The last thing we need to add is a **move** node to the home base. Set the move target to **"gameBase"** (RAIN requires the quotes), and as we want the ship to return home faster than it patrols, change the speed to 10. And since we want the ship to stop as soon as it is near the base, change the **Repeat** dropdown to **Until Success** and set a **Close Enough** distance to 0.1. This will make the ship go to the **gameBase** target and stop. The screen should look as shown:

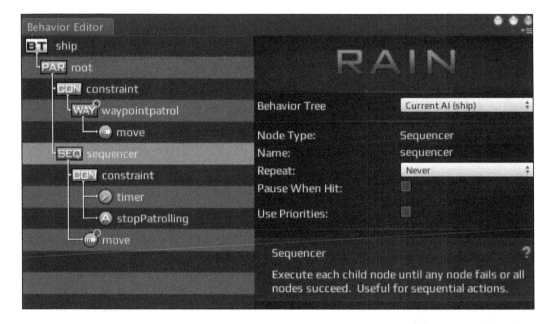

If we run the demo now, the ship will patrol for 5 seconds and then just stop again. The issue here is the **Sequencer** node: it goes through its children returning on the first fail. After the **stopPatrolling** node is activated, the **constraint** nodes will return failure, so when the sequencer calls, it stops after the first constraint. To remedy this, right-click on the **sequencer** node and change its type to **Selector** and rename it to **selector**.

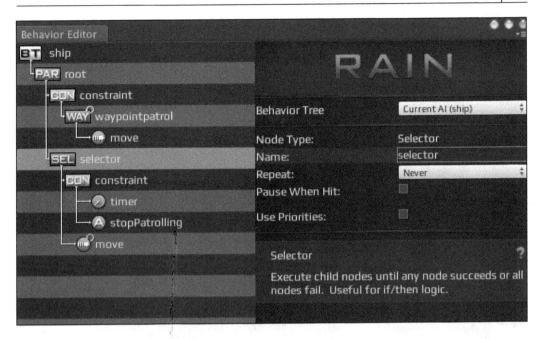

As you can see in the preceding screenshot, recalling the **selector** node works by going through its children returning on the first success instead of failure. So, after patrolling is done and the **constraint** node under the selector returns `false`, instead of the tree stopping, the **move** node can be called. If you run the demo now, everything should work as expected: the ship will patrol for 5 seconds and then quickly return to the game base as shown:

If you didn't end up with this result, try not to get frustrated. Setting up behavior trees is pretty precise, and a misnamed variable or wrong node placement will cause interruptions.

If things are not working for you, open the RAIN behavior tree editor while the game is running (or paused). It will highlight the nodes with red for failure, green for success, and yellow for running:

This is how the RAIN behavior tree editor will display the status of all the nodes.

Summary

In this chapter, we went through the most popular way to set up behaviors for game entities and behavior trees. We went through the process of defining behaviors, deciding the different actions the behaviors will perform and the transitions between the actions. Then, we set up a character and run the game. This is the process to create logic for your game characters, deciding what the behaviors are and the different conditions that can cause them to become active.

In the next chapter, we will look at how to use behavior trees more with character movement and see how to set up the wander behavior for crowd creation. We will explore AIs that will control a large collection of NPCs moving in distinctly separate low-repeating paths.

4
Crowd Chaos

Part of having a realistic game environment is having the nonplayer characters and NPCs act in a believable way. Crowd chaos is all about keeping NPCs busy to create crowded backgrounds for our games. Perhaps your game is set up in a mall, or a city, or any other place where lots of NPCs need to wander around and look like they are doing something. Crowds like these will be the subject of this chapter and the next.

In this chapter, you will learn about:

- Working with crowd chaos
- How to create crowd type characters in the React and RAIN AI packages
- Expanding our knowledge of behavior trees

An overview of crowd chaos

Crowd Chaos is all about giving separate interests to a large number of NPCs, so they look like they are living their own lives. In its lightest form, this can be something very simple, such as a whole bunch of NPCs picking random targets, walking to them, possibly sitting still for a moment, and then starting over. This stands out in real-time strategy games when buildings are constructed, and you see a construction worker walking to random points of the structure and waving their arms about.

Every game that needs crowd chaos will typically have a basic wandering base, and it can be extended as needed. Perhaps the crowd will form lines of more NPCs that are waiting at a spot. Perhaps the targets have changing values and AIs prefer higher values. They pick up a random block and put it somewhere else. The base wandering behavior needed for these and other crowd behaviors is what we will implement in both React and RAIN AI.

React AI

For this demo, we will duplicate the path-following behavior demo in React from *Chapter 1*, *Pathfinding*, and then update it to see some emergent behavior develop from it. We will need to complete the following:

- Create a world with some walls
- Create target markers in the scene
- Create a script with a custom editor to find the targets
- Create the behavior
- Create NPCs and assign the behavior

Setting up a scene with React

To start out with, we will need a basic environment for characters to walk in. Create a plane, call it **Floor**, and add some cubes, shaping them into walls. These will need to be static so that Unity's navigation mesh can find them. Then, we'll need to select the floor and add the navigation mesh. If you've forgotten how to do any of this, it is all covered in the React tutorial in *Chapter 1*, *Pathfinding*.

Next, we need some targets. We'll use a different approach for this from our previous demos and let GameObjects mark the targets. Create an empty GameObject and call it **Targets**. Underneath it, add more empty GameObjects. Give them all a tag, `NpcActivityTarget`, which you might need to create. Distribute these targets to different locations on the screen like this:

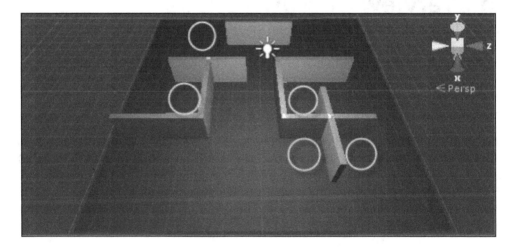

The preceding screenshot shows how our basic React scene setup with targets should look like.

Now, we need a script that can find these locations. It will be based on our earlier scripts and will contain three methods: one to find a target, one to move to a target, and another to hang around.

You can find the completed script at **Disk | Scripts | React AI | LookBusy.cs**. To get the tags to show up as a dropdown, we've also provided a custom editor, which is also available at **Disk | Scripts | React AI | TagOption.cs**. You will need to put this under `Assets/Editor` for it to work in Unity. **TagOptions** is a script that does nothing more than give a drop-down selector for the tag to be used. **LookBusy** uses the selected tag to find objects that are targets in the game.

Here are a couple of the methods inside the script. These are easy to reproduce or modify on your own:

```
GameObject[] targets = GameObject.FindGameObjectsWithTag(this.
SelectedTag);
// If there are not at least two targets to choose from return an
error
if(targets.Length < 2)
{
   Debug.LogWarning("LookBusy.cs:FindTarget() --> There are less than
2 targets with the tag, '" + this.SelectedTag + "'. This script wants
more positions.");
   yield return NodeResult.Failure;
   yield break;
}
// From the targets randomly select one and if it is closer than our
minimum distance return it, otherwise keep trying a constant number of
times before failing
int attempts = 0;

while(Vector3.Distance(this.Destination.transform.position, this.
transform.position) < this.MinimumDistance)
{
   this.Destination = targets[Random.Range(0, targets.Length)];
if(attempts >= 25)
{
    Debug.LogWarning("LookBusy.cs:FindTarget() --> Could not find a
target farther than the mininum distance. Either lower the mininum
distance or space the targets farther apart.");
    yield return NodeResult.Failure;
   }
}
yield return NodeResult.Success;
}
```

In this script, we first check whether we have at least two targets in the game tagged to select from, and if we don't have them, the script reports an error. You'll notice that the error doesn't break the game, it just gives a specific warning on the log of what you need and where the log was posted from. Next, the script selects a random position from the list of nodes, and if the position within a character's minimum distance (and not the same target the character is already on), the script returns the position. This random position is chosen from the list of nodes no more than a constant number of times, that is, 25 times. This random choosing method doesn't guarantee success, but it is a quick and easy way to choose a random target.

Besides picking a random place for a character to walk to, we also need a random amount of time for the NPC to stay at the location they go to. The `HangAround` method does this:

```
public Action HangAround()
{
  // Choose a random time to wait
  float randomtime = Random.Range(this.ShortWaitTime, this.
LongWaitTime);
  while(totalTime < randomtime)
  {
    totalTime += UnityEngine.Time.deltaTime;
    yield return NodeResult.Continue;
  }
  totalTime = 0;
  yield return NodeResult.Success;
}
```

The `HangAround` function just makes us wait a few seconds. First, it selects how long to wait, and then, once this amount of time passes, returns a success. Notice that we return `NodeResult.Continue`. This tells the script to wait until the next update and then try to get, then see if it is finished yet. (Yield is used so the game doesn't freeze up.)

The `MoveToTarget` function isn't given here as it is nearly identical to the function we used in *Chapter 1, Pathfinding*, except that now we are going after the target specified randomly from `FindTarget`.

Building behavior trees in React

Now that we have our behavior methods, we can build the behavior tree. Right-click on your project's `Assets` folder and navigate to **Create | Reactable**. Rename it to `LookBusyReactable`. Then, right-click on it and select **Edit Reactable**:

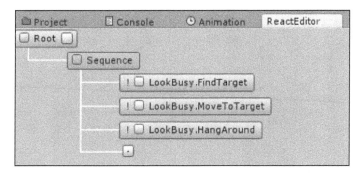

The preceding is a screenshot of the behavior tree editor completed. Right-click on **Root** and navigate to **Add | Branch | Sequence**. This is so it completes each step before moving on to the next. Right-click on **Sequence** and navigate to **Add | Leaf | Action**. Do this three times:

1. For the first one, click on the empty checkbox and navigate to **Scripts | LookBusy | FindTarget**. This is part of the `LookBusy.cs` script that we added earlier.

2. For the second one, do the same but instead navigate to **Scripts | LookBusy | MoveToTarget**.

3. For the third one, navigate to **Scripts | LookBusy | HangAround**.

The AI will find a random target from the list of GameObjects with the correct tag, **NpcActivityTarget**, as we set in the `LookBusy` script. Then, it moves to that target and hangs around for 2 to 4 seconds.

Setting up wandering characters with React

Finally, we will create the NPCs and assign a behavior. For this, you can use a character similar to the first, just a sphere stretch 2x tall, with a small cube on the front of it so that we can see the direction it is facing. Add the LookBusy script to the NPC:

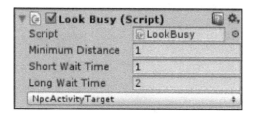

This is how the LookBusy script options look like.

Minimum Distance is how far away you can be from the target and still be satisfied that you reached it. **Short Wait Time** and **Long Wait Time** are time ranges (in seconds) you hang around for, and **NpcActivityTarget** is the tag that the GameObjects have to identify as targets.

Next, add **Nav Mesh Agent** to the NPC so that it can navigate around the level. Finally, add the Reactor script and set its **Reactable** property to **LookBusyReactable**, which is the behavior tree we created earlier.

This completes all the steps needed to have NPC characters wander around in a game using React. You should now be able to create as many characters as you like and have them walk around a level.

RAIN AI

We have already looked at a basic wander behavior for RAIN in *Chapter 2, Patrolling*, when creating patrolling AI, but there, we manually created each possible location for the NPC to go to. In this demo, we will pick random points to wander to from anywhere in the navigation mesh. The NPCs won't have any interaction, though such features are not difficult to add. Here is a breakdown of the steps we will do in this section:

- Set up a world
- Build the behavior tree
- Add a script to pick new points
- Add the NPCs
- Learn about the RAIN AI world and behavior tree setup

First, we'll create a new world. Start with a large plane called `floor`, and add some cubes shaped into walls. You will need to add a navigation mesh and bake it into the scene. These are the same steps we have performed for RAIN demos in earlier chapters. The following is an example of how the scene could look:

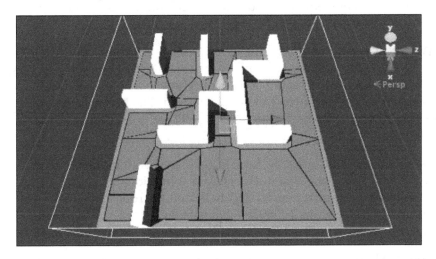

Next comes the behavior tree. From the RAIN menu, select **Behavior Tree Editor**. Create a new tree called `RandomWalk`. The objective of this AI is broken into three steps, taken in this order: select a target, walk to it, and then wait a moment. This is a good case for the RAIN decision node sequenced. Under the root node, we will right-click and go to **Create | Decisions | Sequencer**.

As there is no behavior tree node built into RAIN that will choose a random location, we will use a custom action and write our own script. Right-click on the new SEQ node and navigate to **Create | Actions | Custom Action**. Set the **Repeat** property to **Until Success** because we want it to continue processing this node until it returns a success and then move on to the next node. Name the custom action node `Select Next Target`. You'll notice that you can put spaces in the name. This is useful as it shows up in the behavior tree, making it easier to follow:

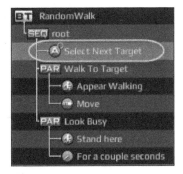

We could add the script now, but we'll finish the rest of the nodes in the tree and then come back; for now, we will assume that the script will find a spot to walk to. The next action is to walk to it. This needs two things happening simultaneously, animation and actual walking, which means that we will use the **Parallel** decision node. Right-click on the sequence node and select **Create | Decisions | Parallel**. Name it **Walk to Target**.

Under **Walk to Target**, right-click and go to **Create | Actions | Animate**. Name it `Appear Walking`. Set the animation state to **walk**. Also under **Walk to Target**, right-click and navigate to **Create | Actions | Move**. Name it `Move`. Set the **Move Speed** property to 1, so it moves 1 meter per second. The **Move Target** value should be set to **TargetPoint** without the quotes. **TargetPoint** doesn't exist yet; our script will create it.

The last step that the NPC must perform is generate a wait moment. To give the NPC more life, we will make sure that it uses an idle animation, which also means two things must happen simultaneously. Right-click on the root sequence node (**SEQ**) and go to **Create | Decisions | Parallel**. Name it `Look Busy`. Add an animation action under this and set **idle** as its **Animation State** and **Stand here** as its name.

Also, under the **Look Busy** node, we will right-click and go to **Create | Actions | Wait for Timer**. Name it `For a couple seconds`. Set the **Seconds** property to **2**.

The behavior tree is now complete. All we need to do now is fill in the script that gets our **TargetPoint**, so it knows where to move.

RAIN AI custom wander scripts

To start creating our needed wander scripts, first select the **Select Next Target** action in the behavior tree. Under the **Class** property, set it to **Create Custom Action**, which pops up a box to define the script. The following screenshot shows what a RAIN custom action creation dialog looks like:

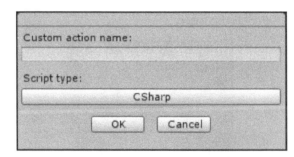

Set the name to `SelectRandomTarget` and the script to **CSharp**. This will generate the default custom action script file already filled with a few common methods. In this demo, we only need to use the `Execute` function:

```
public override ActionResult Execute(AI ai)
{
  var loc = Vector3.zero;
  List<RAINNavigationGraph> found = new List<RAINNavigationGraph>();
  do
  {
    loc = ai.Kinematic.Position;
    loc.x += Random.Range(-8f, 8f);
    loc.z += Random.Range(-8f, 8f);
    found = NavigationManager.Instance.GraphsForPoints(
      ai.Kinematic.Position,
      loc,
      ai.Motor.StepUpHeight,
      NavigationManager.GraphType.Navmesh,
      ((BasicNavigator)ai.Navigator).GraphTags);
  }
  while ( Vector3.Distance(loc, ai.Kinematic.Position) < 2f
      || found.Count == 0);
  ai.WorkingMemory.SetItem<Vector3>("TargetPoint", loc);
  return ActionResult.SUCCESS;
}
```

In this code, we try to find a good value for the `loc` variable, a location variable that is set to a different random location, up to 18 meters away. The `found` variable identifies whether a path exists or not. These two things are determined in a loop, which ends as long as two conditions are met. First, the distance has to be greater than 2, as the movement should be detected by the player and second, we see if the points found is greater than zero. If it found none, then we would not be able to get to that location.

Once the `loc` variable has a location that works, the next thing it does is use RAIN's memory system and sets a memory entry, **TargetPoint**, to the new location. Remember that we have the **Move** action in our behavior set to find **TargetPoint**, so **Move** will go to our newly found location. Finally, we return a success.

This completes our behavior and script. The last thing we need to do is give that behavior to some NPCs and run the game.

Putting NPCs in the RAIN demo

Start by adding another simple NPC character to the game, like we did in the first chapter. We don't need to add any scripts directly to it. Instead, make sure that the NPC is selected in the hierarchy, and from the RAIN menu, select **Create AI**.

In the AI GameObject/component that was added, from the **Mind** tab, set the **Behavior Tree Asset** value to **RandomWalk**, which is found in **Assets**. Under the animation tab, click on the **Add Existing Animations** button.

Now, try the game. A single NPC should be walking around the screen, pausing, and then walking to another location at random. To create a larger crowd, just duplicate the NPC GameObject in the scene at several locations.

Summary

We were able to use scripting and behavior trees in both React AI and RAIN to effectively create a wandering AI. Each AI had strengths and weaknesses, though the weaknesses were more of a preference.

Behavior tree editors were used in both RAIN and React, and both work in a similar fashion. In RAIN, you can start editing a tree from the menu, or from the editor itself. (It had the option to select the behavior directly in the editor.) With React, you can do this from the **Project** tab, by right-clicking and choosing to edit it. React had premade scripts that can do nearly all the actions that were needed, except that instead of selecting randomly from a list of targets with the tag, it would select a target expecting only one object with that tag. With RAIN, we made a custom action node to choose a location to go to.

Both React and RAIN AI are general AI systems that are useful for many different types of game situations, so neither were designed specifically to handle crowds. In the next chapter, we will look at different tools with more focus on creating crowd AI.

5
Crowd Control

In this chapter, you will learn how to build large crowds into your game. Instead of having the crowd members wander freely, like we did in the previous chapter, we will control the crowds better by giving them directions on what to do. This material will be useful for a wide range of game use cases, such as planning soldier attacks by groups or directing flows of traffic in a car game.

In this chapter, you will learn about:

- Crowd-steering behaviors
- Using the Fame Crowd Simulation API to manage crowds
- Exploring ANT-Op to create more goal-directed crowds

An overview of crowd control

In *Chapter 4*, *Crowd Chaos*, we looked at creating crowds using wandering behaviors, where different crowd members worked individually to travel to different points. This works well for ambient crowds, but there was no working as a group. As there was no larger group-defined behavior or director managing crowds, our previous implementations required creating and configuring character AIs individually. Defining and configuring individual AIs is fine for smaller groups, but not practical when creating much larger crowds. In the demos in this chapter, we will look at crowds that work, or at least move, as a group. Moving AI characters in groups, also called flocks, has been a popular subject in AI for many years. The most popular system is called **Boids**, and it was designed in the 1980s by Craig Reynolds, a renowned computer graphics and AI developer, and the basic design is used in crowd AIs in most games today. In these systems, different simple steering behaviors are defined, such as moving to a target position or following a path, as well as behaviors to not collide with other agents or align to the same direction of nearby agents.

These simple behaviors are applied to large numbers of game characters (or in the original system, Boids), and when they run together, they move as groups the way you would expect them to. These simple behavior combinations give surprisingly realistic results considering how simple the individual steering behaviors are.

Steering algorithms are simple to implement, but instead of coding something from scratch, we will use Unity plugins. The two plugins we will be focusing on, the Fame Crowd Simulation API and ANT-Op, are not general-purpose AI systems like RAIN; instead, they are focused just on crowd management. This is a popular trend in the AI world. Sometimes, instead of a large AI system, it's best to look for specific tools for specific AI tasks. Don't worry about combining multiple AI subsystems while designing the AI for your games, as this can often give you the best result.

The Fame Crowd Simulation API focuses, as you might expect, on crowds with a system design similar to Boids. It allows you to customize different values for the various steering behaviors and has a GUI interface that makes forming and directing crowds very straightforward. ANT-Op is based on simulating ants. Looking at ants might sound strange, but ant simulation is actually a popular topic in the AI world, since ants work really well as a group. Both of these plugins are useful when creating controlled crowds.

More details about Craig Reynolds' original flocking and steering systems can be found in his papers online:

- *Steering Behaviors for Autonomous Characters*: http://www.red3d.com/cwr/papers/1999/gdc99steer.html
- *Flocks, Herds, and Schools: A Distributed Behavioral Model*: http://www.red3d.com/cwr/papers/1987/boids.html

The Fame Crowd Simulation API

The Fame Crowd Simulation API by TechBizXccelerator is available at Unity Asset Store under the name Crowd Simulator API for $45 at the time of writing this book. It allows you to create groups and customize steering behaviors. For our crowd demo, we will create a demo with many spaceships traveling in a group.

Setting up a scene with Fame

To create our demo, first create a new scene with a plane as the ground. Like most of the AI plugins in this book, Fame Crowd Simulation also supports Unity's built-in terrain system, but for this demo, a basic ground plane will be fine. Fame also uses a singleton pattern that has one class that manages everything for crowd management, so create an empty GameObject and call it **Crowd Manager**. Then, import Fame if it is not already in your project, and attach the FameManager script from Fame Assets/FameScripts/FameManager.cs to the **Crowd Manager** GameObject. This initial setup is shown in the following screenshot:

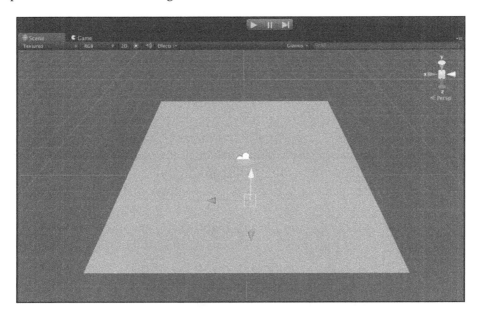

The following should be the hierarchy:

This is our basic Fame scene setup with a **Crowd Manager** object.

The **FameManager** object will be our main point of interaction with Fame, and we can interact with it from anywhere in our game code.

Unlike the other systems we saw where we create the AI characters individually to define our crowds, in Fame, we will define a group of characters, also called a flock. Add the ship model from *Chapter 3, Behavior Trees,* and then create another empty GameObject and call it Ships. Then, attach the FlockGroup.cs script to it from Assets/FrameScripts.

 To avoid the warning about not having a terrain in **FAME settings,** disable **Enable Terrain Effect** in **FameManager** and **Get Info From Terrain GameObject** in Fame terrain.

FlockGroup is the main class to hold a group of characters, and it has several settings we can customize:

- **Flock Type**: This is **Ground** or **Air** and defines whether the AI characters will move on a plane (ground) or move in all three axes (air). If set to **Air**, characters will ignore any terrain. You might think we would set our ships to air, but we want them to all hover at the same height, so keep this set to ground.

- **Num Agent**: This is the number of agents (or AI characters) in the group. This can be a very high number as Fame is efficient, but for our demo, we will set this to 8.

- **Avatar**: This is the GameObject set to be the individual members of the crowd. For our demo, this is the ship model.

- **FlockMemberScript**: You can create a custom script to define how the members of your crowd will act. For this demo, we will keep things simple and use Fame's default FlockMemberScript.cs script.

The following screenshot shows our Fame **FlockGroup** settings for the ship group:

Setting up a group

Next, we need to create the initial formation we want our group to be in. With the **Ships** GameObject selected, you will see three connected gizmos in the Unity 3D view that represent the shape of the initial group. Go to **Formation Shape** in the **Inspector** panel for **Ships** and click on **Add Point**. This creates a fourth point for the shape of the group. Arrange the points into a pyramid-like shape and click on **Create Avatars**. A set of ships in a group will be created:

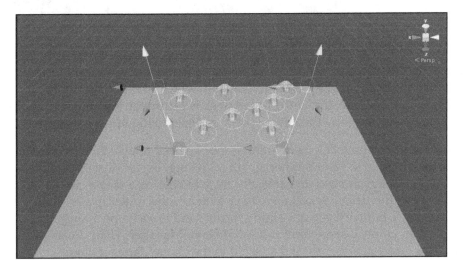

This is our group setup that shows the control points that define the boundary for our group. You can see our ship group shape with eight ships has been created.

Creating a group object was really easy with Fame. Now, we need to set up a way for our crowd to move. We will have the ships move across the plane to a target point. Set the Z scale of the plane to a larger value, create a sphere object to be our target position, and place it across the plane. The screen should look as follows:

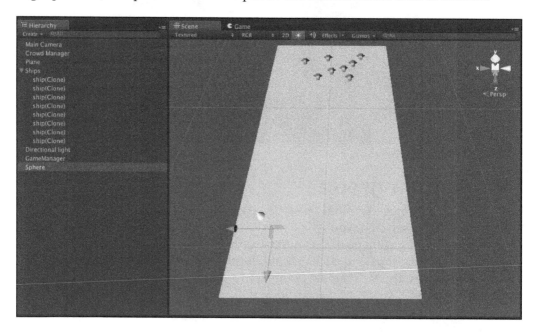

You can see a group of ships with a target placed.

When we send the group, or flock, the command to move to the target location, it will move the position of the flock to match it, which isn't necessarily the center of the flock. In this demo, the center of the flock is the upper-left corner from the camera view, which is why the target sphere is offset to the upper-left corner.

Now that we have a target element in the scene, we need to give Fame a command to move the group to it. Fame supports path following, but as most of the time we will want our groups to move dynamically, such as chasing a player, we will look at how to move the crowd by code. We have a lot of ways to set up a script to control the flock, but we'll take the simplest route and use a game manager. Create another empty GameObject and call it **GameManager**. Then, create a new script, GameManager.cs, and attach it to the **GameManager** object.

Add the following code to it:

```
using UnityEngine;
using System.Collections;

public class GameManager : MonoBehaviour {

  public Transform target;

  void Start () {

  }

  void Update () {
    FlockGroup group = FameManager.GetFlockGroup(1); // Get first
flock

    group.MoveGroupAbs(target.position);
  }
}
```

In this code, we have a public variable for the target for the flock. In the Unity editor, drag the **Sphere** target object to this field to set its value. Then, in the update, we just get the flock group from Fame manager (which is a singleton class with static methods, so we don't need a reference to it). Then, we just use `MoveGroupAbs` that tells the group to move to a specific location. (There is also a method called `MoveGroup` that takes in an offset instead of an absolute position you can use if you want the crowd to move in a general direction instead of to a specific point.) If you run the demo now, the ships will travel down the ground to the target point. As you can see, setting up a crowd and giving directions for it to move is very easy and straightforward with Fame.

Adding obstacles to Fame

Next, let's add an obstacle inbetween the ships and their target. Increase the size of the ground plane by increasing its X scale. Then, add a cylinder to the middle of the scene to be an obstacle for the ships. To have this obstacle recognized by Fame, add the Fame obstacle script, `FameObstacle.cs`, to it. Fame allows two types of obstacles: round (circles) and 2D polygons. You specify the polygon ones, the same as we did for group shapes, by modifying control points. For our obstacle, we just need it to match the radius of the cylinder. In this example, the cylinder has a scale of **50**, which makes its radius 25, so set the obstacle's **radius** to 25.

The demo should now look like the following screenshot:

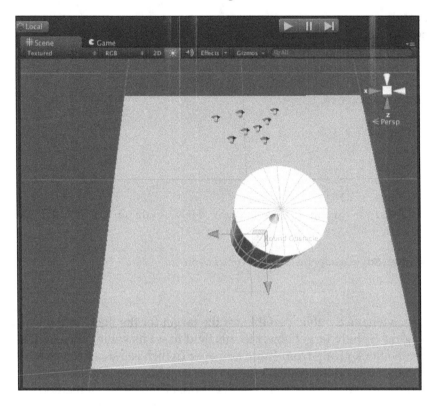

This is the obstacle setup for our ship group.

If you run the demo now, the ships will go to their target and smoothly avoid the obstacle. You can see in the next screenshot how the ships avoid our obstacle:

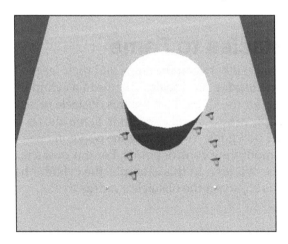

Adding vector fields to Fame

We just saw how to add obstacles to our Fame crowd scene. Right now, all of our ships split when avoiding the cylinder, about half to the left and the other half to the right. However, we want all of them to move to the left. To do this, we can vector fields to the scene. Vector fields are a popular way of adding directional *hints* to a scene, and they are defined areas that have directional vectors that are associated with them. When a character is inside the field, the vector helps move the character in the desired direction. Vector fields can be a powerful tool for level design and are easy to add to your scene. To see how easy it is to add them to the scene, add a new empty GameObject to the scene and name it `Field`. Then, attach the `FameField.cs` script from `Assets/Fame Assets/FameScripts` to it. The field can be rectangular, called **Uniform** or **Circular**. Select **Uniform** for the type and set **x** and **z widths** to **75**. Then, set the angle to **45** and the magnitude to **100**. The white arrow visualizes the angle for the vector field. Place the field over the initial positions for the ships, as shown:

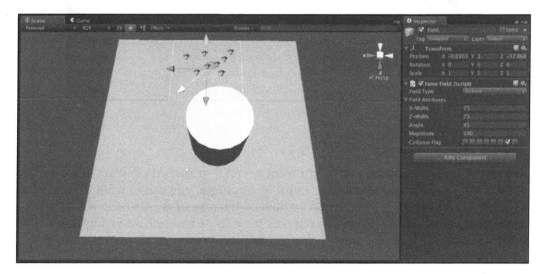

If you run the demo now, ships will all veer to the left before avoiding the cylinder. For larger levels, you can set up multiple vector fields; they are a good way to control the general movement of AI characters.

This Fame demo showed you the basics you'll need to create organized crowds for most games: creating crowds, giving them directions to move, and adding obstacles and vector fields. Next, we will look at another specialized AI plugin, ANT-Op. You can see the ship group changing its direction because of the vector field. You can also notice how our crowd uses the vector fields to direct ship movement to the left:

ANT-Op

Sometimes for your games, you might want to create crowd AIs that act in a very unique way, and instead of using an existing AI plugin, you might want to create a crowd AI from scratch. This would be done in the case of an ANT-Op AI. As we mentioned before, ant behavior is a popular topic in AI research and computer science in general. Initially, ants work independently and give off pheromones that are sensed by other ants to communicate messages. For example, when ants start searching for food, they give off pheromones as they search. When they find food, they give off different pheromones as they bring it back to the colony, which directs the next ants when searching for food. ANT-Op, by Gray Lake Studios, is available on Unity Asset Store for $75, and it simulates this ant food search process. Unlike the other AI plugins in this book, Ant-Op isn't really designed to be brought into an existing game; it's more of a technical demonstration that is a simulation you can use to see interesting AI at work and hopefully use it to inspire complex AI designs for your games. To start the demo, import ANT-Op and double-click on **Test Scene** to open it. The scene will initially be blank, but if you start the demo, you can see the simulation start. In the following screenshot, you can see ANT-Op in action:

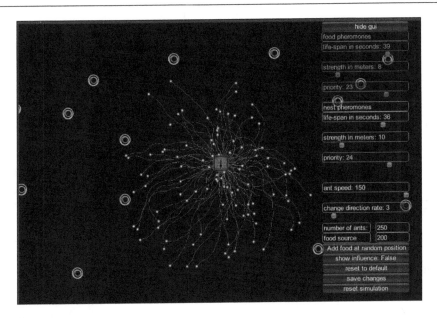

You can see ANT-Op simulating an ant colony. The lines represent pheromones from the ants.

The options on the right are different settings for the simulation. You can play by changing the values, and these can be saved to an XML file for later reloading. Running the simulation provides a complex visualization, which you can see in the following screenshot:

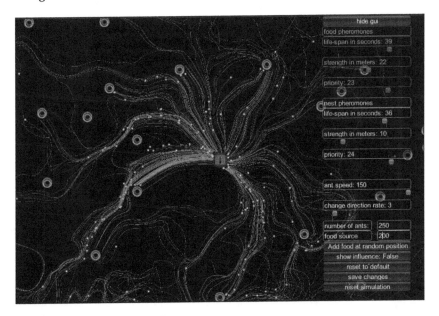

Again, this probably isn't something you would bring into your game as is; it's to generate ideas for your AI. The source files can be reviewed for ideas on creating your own AI. Don't underestimate what you can learn by looking at AI simulations like this.

Summary

This concludes the last of two chapters on crowd AI. Where the previous chapter focused on defining crowds by defining wander behaviors for different characters individually, in this chapter we focused on defining groups as a whole. We discussed steering-based group design and looked at the Fame Crowd Simulation API that you can use to set up crowds easily, give them direction, and have them adjust steering based on other factors in the environment, obstacles, and vector fields. We then discussed defining your own crowd AI for more unique systems and looked at ANT-Op as an example of this. This should give you all the info you need to create all kinds of crowds for your games.

In the next few chapters, we will turn the focus to having AI characters interact with their environment. In *Chapter 6, Sensors and Activities*, we will look at having our characters sense things in the environment and react to them.

6

Sensors and Activities

In the previous chapters on pathfinding and behavior trees, we had AI characters moving through our AI environments and changing states, but they didn't really react to anything. They knew about the navigation mesh and different points in the scene, but there was no way for them to sense different objects in the game and react to them. This chapter changes that; we will look at how to tag objects in the game so that our characters can sense and react to them.

In this chapter, you will learn about:

- Sensors and tagging game objects so that they can be sensed
- AI characters that use sensors in RAIN
- Advanced configuration of sensors in RAIN
- Having AI characters react to different objects and perform different activities once they are sensed

An overview of sensing

A part of having good game AI is having the AI characters react to other parts of the game in a realistic way. For example, let's say you have an AI character in a scene searching for something, such as the player to attack them or items to collect (as in the demo in this chapter). We could have a simple proximity check, for example, if the enemy is 10 units from the player, it starts attacking. However, what if the enemy wasn't looking in the direction of the player and wouldn't be able to see or hear the player in real life? Having the enemy attack then is very unrealistic. We need to be able to set up more realistic and configurable sensors for our AI.

To set up senses for our characters, we will use RAIN's senses system. You might assume that we will use standard methods to query a scene in Unity, such as performing picking through Unity's ray casting methods. This works for simple cases, but RAIN has several advanced features to configure sensors for more realism. The senses RAIN supports are seeing and hearing. They are defined as volumes attached to an object, and the AI might be able to sense objects only inside the volume. Not everything in the volume can be sensed because there might be additional restrictions such as not being able to see through walls. A visualization illustrates this volume in the editor view to make configuring them easier. The following figure is based on the visualization of a sense in a RAIN AI:

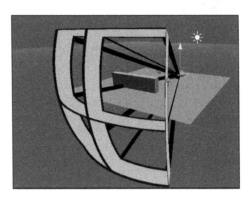

 The early versions of RAIN included additional senses, such as smell, with the idea that more senses meant more realism. However, adding more senses was confusing for users and was used only in rare cases, so they were cut from the current versions. If you need a sense such as smell for something like the ant demo we saw in *Chapter 5, Crowd Control*, try modifying how you use vision or hearing, such as using a visual for smell and have it on a layer not visible to players in game.

While setting up characters to sense game objects in their environment, you might think that the AI system would automatically analyze everything in the scene (game objects and geometry) to determine what is sensed. This will work for small levels but as we've seen before, we run into the problem of scaling if we have a very large scene with many objects. Larger scenes will mostly have background items that our AI doesn't care about, and we will need a more complex system to analyze all the objects to be efficient. Typically, AI systems work using a simplified version of the level, for example, how pathfinding uses navigation meshes to find a path instead of using the geometry from the level directly because it is much more efficient. Similarly, our senses don't work on everything; for an object to be sensed, it needs to be tagged.

In RAIN, the AI characters we create have an `AIRig` object, but for items we want to detect in the scene, we add a RAIN **Entity** component to them. The **RAIN** menu in Unity has a **Create Entity** option that is used to add an **Entity** component. The tags that you can set on the entities are called **aspects**, and the two types of aspects correspond to our two sensor types: visual aspects and audio aspects. So, a typical workflow to make your AI characters sense the environment is to put **Entity** components on game objects to detect, add aspects to those entities with the different tags a sensor can detect, and create sensors on your AI characters. We will look at a demo of this, but first let's discuss sensors in detail.

Advanced visual sensor settings

We've heard stories of people setting up their sensors — especially visual ones — and starting the game, but nothing happens or it seems to work incorrectly. Configuring the senses' advanced settings can help avoid issues such as these and make development easier.

To see visual sensor settings, add a RAIN AI to a game object and click on the eye icon, select **Visual Sensor** from the **Add Sensor** dropdown, and then click on the gear icon in the upper-right corner and select **Show Advanced Settings**. The following screenshot shows the **Visual Sensor** section in RAIN:

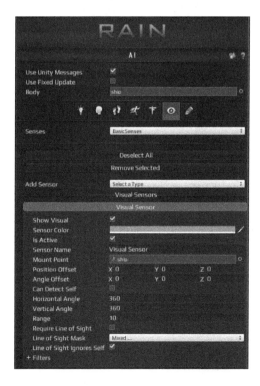

Here are some of the properties of the sensor:

- **Show Visual / Sensor Color**: These are used to show how the sensor will look in the Unity editor, not in the game.

- **Is Active**: This flag determines whether the sensor is currently trying to sense aspects in the scene or whether it is disabled.

- **Sensor Name**: This shows the name of the sensor. This is useful when using the sensor in behavior trees, which we will see in this chapter's demo.

- **Mount Point**: This is the game object the sensor is attached to.

- **Horizontal Angle / Vertical Angle / Range**: These three define the volume of the sense; nothing outside of it will be picked up. The visualization of the sense matches these dimensions. You will want to customize these settings for different characters in your game. Unexpected behavior can occur from setting these up incorrectly.

- **Require Line of Sight**: This flag requires a line from the character to the aspect without intersecting other objects for the aspect to be seen. Without this flag, a character could appear to have X-Ray vision.

- **Can Detect Self / Line of Sight Ignores Self**: These flag if the sensor should ignore the AI character. This is important as it prevents a common problem. For example, we can have several soldier characters with a soldier aspect and then add a soldier from a different team that attacks the other soldiers. However, the attacking soldier when sensing might pick up its own aspect and try to start attacking itself, and this is definitely not what we want.

- **Line of Sight Mask**: To further help control what can be seen, layer masks can be used. These work the same as Unity's ray casting masks.

Advanced audio sensor settings

The properties for the audio sensor is similar to that of the visual sensor, except it doesn't have any line of sight properties and the volume of the sense is a radius and doesn't have vertical or horizontal angle limits. The important properties are:

- **Range**: This specifies how far the sensor can detect

- **Volume Threshold**: When listening for aspects, this is the lowest volume that the sensor can hear

Now that we understand all of our sensor options, let's start the demo.

Using senses with RAIN

For this demo, we will use RAIN 2.14 and have a ship that patrols a path, looks for pieces of gold, and picks them up. To start, we'll use a setup similar to that of the demo in *Chapter 3, Behavior Trees*. You can start from there or recreate it; we just need a ship, a wall, a path, with the ground being a little larger, and the objects spread out a little.

 When changing the base geometry of your game levels, you need to regenerate the navigation mesh. This is done by selecting the **Navigation Mesh** object in your scene and clicking on the **Generate NavMesh** button.

Here is our basic setup. The following image shows the starting point of our sensor demo:

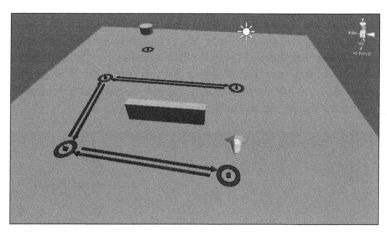

We also just need the behavior tree for the ship to only patrol the path. Set up this behavior like we did in *Chapter 2, Patrolling*, or if you are using the behavior tree demo, delete the timer node functionality. The new behavior tree should look like the following screenshot:

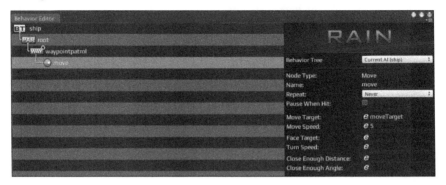

This will be the starting point of the behavior tree for our sensor demo. If you start the demo now, the ship will just keep circling the wall.

Setting up aspects in RAIN

For our sensor demo, we will have the ship look for gold, which will be represented by a simple game object. Create a **Sphere** object in Unity by navigating to **Game Object** | **Create Other** | **Sphere**. Make it a little smaller by giving it **Scale** of **0.25** for **X**, **Y**, and **Z**, and change the material to a golden color. We'll be duplicating the object later so if you want duplicating to be easier, make it a prefab. This is our starting point, as illustrated in the following screenshot:

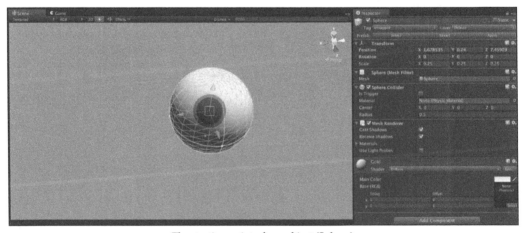

The starting point of our object (Sphere)

To have an aspect, the game object needs an **Entity** component. With **Gold** selected, go to **RAIN | Create Entity**. There are a few settings to customize, but for now just change the **Entity Name** field to **Gold**. The other important setting is **Form**, which is the game object attached to it; we can leave it to **Sphere**.

Click on the **Add Aspect** dropdown and select **Visual Aspect**. Set the aspect name to **Gold** as well. The setting should look like the following screenshot:

We now have an entity with a visual aspect. Create a **Prefab** tab for this **Gold** object and then add it to the opposite side of the wall as the ship. The scene should look like the following screenshot:

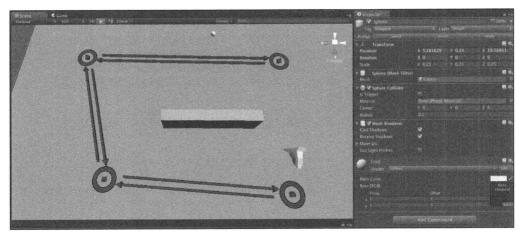

A sensor demo with gold

Setting up a visual sensor in RAIN

We have the gold aspect; next we need a visual sensor. Select **Ship AI**, click on the eye icon for the sensors tab, and from the **Add Sensor** dropdown, select **Visual Sensor**. Go to the **Advanced Settings** (selecting the gear icon) icon and adjust the horizontal and vertical angles as well as the range until the sensor can see a bit in front of the ship. Typically, you will make these very large so that the character can see most of the level. For this demo, the sensor values are **120** for **Horizontal Angle**, **45** for **Vertical Angle**, and **15** for **Range**. Also, check the **Require Line of Sight** option so that the ship can't see gold through the wall. The setup should look like the following screenshot:

If you run the demo now, you will see the ship moving with the sensor (in **Editor View**). The ship with a visual sensor should look like the following image:

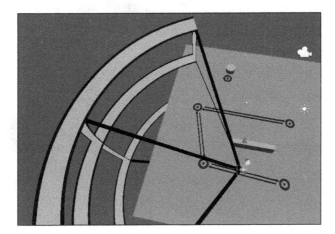

This completes setting up the sensor for our ship.

Changing activities based on sensing

We now have the ship sensing the gold as it passes by, but it still doesn't react to it. To do this, we will update the behavior tree for the ship.

The first thing we want is a detect node as the ship is moving so it can know if it sees **Gold**. Open the behavior tree for the ship and create a detect node. As the detect node will be running continuously, change its **Repeat** type to **Forever** and right-click on the root node and change its type to **Parallel**. For the detection part of the detect node to work, set the **Aspect** field to "Gold" and set the sensor it will be using to "**Visual Sensor**". Finally, we need to set the form of the aspect, the game object attached. Set **Form Variable** to **gold**.

> The whole quotes thing in RAIN can be confusing: why some fields need quotes and others don't. This is planned to be improved in future versions of RAIN, but for now for Expressions (fields with the little e symbol) a value with quotes means the name of an object and without means the value of a variable. So in our case, "**Visual Sensor**" and "**Gold**" were both in quotes as they were referring to objects by name, but **gold** is an actual variable we store data in, so it doesn't have quotes.

Your setup should look like the following screenshot:

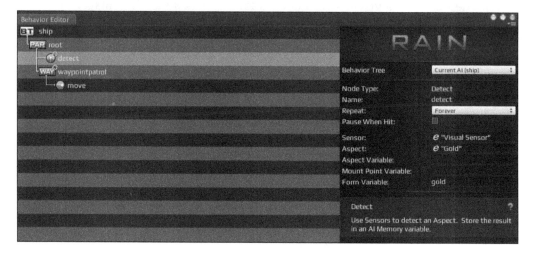

In the preceding screenshot, you can see the behavior tree with the **detect** node.

Now if you run the game, the gold will be detected, but the ship still doesn't move to it yet. To do this, we will use a selector node similar to the original behavior tree demo. Place a **selector** node under root and create a **constraint** node as a child with a **Constraint** value of **gold == null**. Then, move the original patrol node to be a child of the constraint. The setup should look the following screenshot:

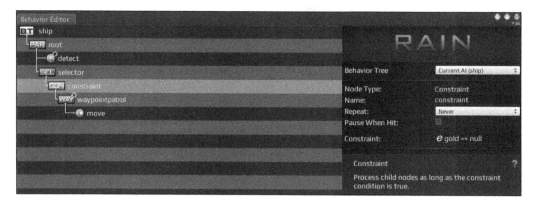

The preceding screenshot shows a detection behavior tree with a **constraint** node.

Now if you run the demo, when the ship sees the gold, the gold value will not be null and it will stop moving. However, instead of stopping, we want it to move over to the gold; so, add another constraint node with the **Expressiongold != null** value and a **move** node below it that has a **Move Target** value of **gold**. Here is how the behavior tree with the **detect** node settings will look:

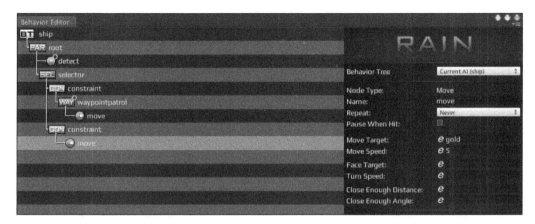

If you run the demo now, the ship will move to the gold when it sees it. However, let's change this so that the ship goes back to patrolling after the pickup. Make sure that both root and selector nodes are set to **Forever** for their **Repeat** type. Then, create a new custom action node (like in *Chapter 3, Behavior Trees*) and put it under the move node for the gold. Create a new class for the custom action and call it `PickUpGold`. Set its code to this:

```
using UnityEngine;
using RAIN.Core;
using RAIN.Action;

[RAINAction]
public class PickUpGold : RAINAction
{
    public PickUpGold()
    {
        actionName = "PickUpGold";
    }

    public override void Start(AI ai)
    {
```

```
        base.Start(ai);

        GameObject gold =
        ai.WorkingMemory.GetItem<GameObject>("gold");

        ai.WorkingMemory.SetItem<GameObject>("gold", null);

        Object.Destroy(gold);
    }

    public override ActionResult Execute(AI ai)
    {
        return ActionResult.SUCCESS;
    }

    public override void Stop(AI ai)
    {
        base.Stop(ai);
    }
}
```

The important code here is in the `Start` method. We got the `gold` game object that was sensed from the memory and then erased it from memory by setting the `gold` value to `null`. Then, we destroyed the `gold` object, so it won't be sensed anymore. If you run the code now, the ship will follow the path, pick up gold when it sees it, and then go back to the path.

Next, try adding several more gold prefabs to the scene and run the demo, as shown in the following image:

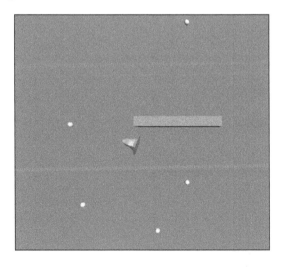

Now in the demo, the ship will go and collect all the different gold pieces it sees and then return to the path.

RAIN sensor filters

If you tried running the demo with multiple gold pieces, you must have seen a small problem. The ship always goes to the first piece of gold it sees, but that might not be the closest. If it sees a distant piece from the corner of its eye, it will go straight to it even if there are ones closer to it. A quick fix for this is to add a filter to the RAIN sensors. Filters are ways to manipulate the list of sensed objects, and RAIN might have more in the future but for now, it just has one: **NearestXFilter**. Select **Visual Sensor** in the ship and set the **Size** field to **1** and select **NearestXFilter** under the **Filters** section. The following screenshot will show the settings of **NearestXFilter** on the sensor:

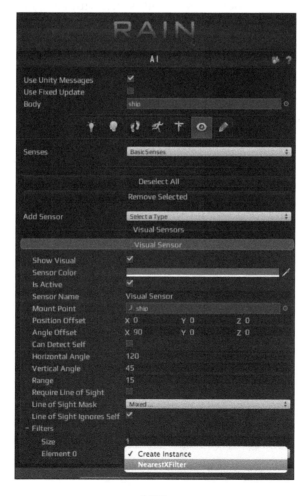

The **NearestXFilter** filter will send a given number of closest objects to the sensor. In our case, we just leave it to one. If you run the demo now, the ship will always pick up the gold that it can see and that is the closest to it first. This completes our ship demo.

Summary

In this chapter, we looked at how to set up sensors for our AI characters so that they can see the environment. We also saw how to tag objects with aspects so that they are visible to our AI. We also saw how to change a character's activities based on sensing, and we discussed different settings for sensors and how to tweak them. Sensors and aspects can make your game's AI more realistic, but they need to be carefully adjusted to give good results.

In the next chapter, we will look at taking our work with navigation and mind development to make our characters react more to their environments. Specifically, we will see how all of the AI we have used so far can make our AI characters adapt to different game events and create more complex AI.

7
Adaptation

Having good AI for our characters is more than just giving them simple tasks to perform; we'd like to have our characters realistically react to the game environment. Game events such as seeing new objects appear or having a bomb go off in a scene should cause a reaction in the AI. Having the AI adapt to the environment is a huge topic, but we will focus on the basic ways to have AI adapt to the environment. In this chapter, we will look at taking AI skills we learned in previous chapters and combining them to create AI characters that adapt to the game environment in a realistic way, changing their tasks based on game events.

In this chapter, you will be:

- Creating AI characters that react and adapt to multiple game events
- Setting up more complex AI characters in RAIN
- Getting to know the importance of creating larger AI scenes with REACT AI

An overview

In previous chapters, we looked at how to do different specific AI tasks. We learned how to make characters patrol a path, have them wander an environment, change state with behavior trees, and sense objects in the game environment. These are all important, but it's more important to understand how we can combine these different elements to make AI that works well in a large game environment. We will need characters that can navigate an environment to perform tasks but then change based on game events that occur. To do this, the game needs to be designed at a high level, defining what the different AI character's main goals and actions are. These high-level goals are things such as wanting an enemy to patrol an area until it sees the player and then start to chase and attack him. From there, the different aspects of sensing need to be designed for the level, deciding what objects need to be tagged, so they can be used by the AI system. The characters then need sensors defined for the AI characters and high-level goals can be created using existing nodes and custom actions.

One of the ways we can define our character's adaptive behavior with RAIN is using RAIN's motor system. We have been using the motor system with the move node but not directly. The motor system controls moving the character, and it is available through the motion panel in RAIN, the icon with two feet. This is how the motion panel in RAIN looks:

RAIN supports three different kinds of motors:

- A basic motor, which we will use for most cases
- A character controller that uses the standard Unity character controller for movement
- A Mecanim controller (we will discuss Mecanim with RAIN in *Chapter 10, Animation and AI*)

The movement is target based: you give the motor a target position to go to and use the motor to get there.

> Unity's character controller is very popular, but if you want to use it with RAIN, stick with RAIN's character controller. There are some known issues mixing Unity's basic character controller and RAIN 2.1.4. These should be fixed in a future version.

The fields for motors are pretty straightforward:

- **Speed / Rotation Speed**: This specifies how fast the character should move and rotate.

- **Close Enough Distance / Close Enough Angle**: This specifies how close the character needs to move to a target.

- **Face Before Move Angle**: This specifies how much of an angle the character needs to be facing its target before moving. This prevents weird movements with very close targets.

- **Step Up Height**: This specifies how much the character can step up; this is used to customize behavior for things such as steep terrain and staircases. We will discuss step up heights more in *Chapter 11, Advanced NavMesh Generation*.

We use the motor system from a **Custom Action** option in our demo, but you can use motors to move the character from any component.

Here's a little snippet that shows how to move from a standard Unity character script:

```
AIRigaiRig = GetComponentInChildren<AIRig>();
...
aiRig.AI.Motor.UpdateMotionTransforms();

aiRig.AI.Motor.MoveTarget.VectorTarget = targetPositon;
aiRig.AI.Motor.Move();
aiRig.AI.Motor.ApplyMotionTransforms();
```

First, we get `AIRig` attached to the character. Then, we call `UpdateMotionTransforms()` to make sure that the AI system has the latest transforms (position and rotation) from the character before updating. Next, we set `VectorTarget` to a `Vector3` variable as `targetPosition`, so the AI system knows where we want to go. Then, we call `Move()` to update the character's transforms in the AI system, and finally, we call `ApplyMotionTransforms()` to update our game to show the new transforms from the AI system. Using these methods, we can update game characters at any time.

With customized movements, we can have our characters adapt in any way we want. The best way to see how this works is to look at a demo. The demo that we will look at in this chapter is an extension of the ship demo from *Chapter 6, Sensors and Activities*. We will have a ship in a level searching for gold pieces, but we'll extend it to make the gold pieces appear more random and dynamic in the level over time. Then, we will have a bomb with a timer and when it goes off all of ships will be destroyed and stop updating their AI. This will illustrate how we can have AI characters react to game events.

RAIN's demo

The basic start of the demo will be similar to our others, a ground with several walls around for our ships to travel. This is how the basic starting point of our demo should look:

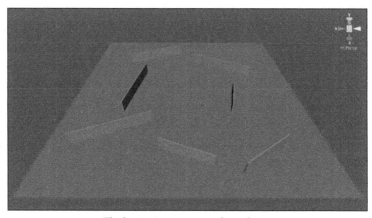

The basic starting point of our demo

One of the first things we will need is the ability to query a random location in the scene to spawn and find points to travel to. Create a class called Ground and add it to the ground plane. This class will be used to provide higher-level information about the level, the first of which is being able to find a random position in the level. Here is the Ground class with the random position chooser method:

```
using UnityEngine;
using System.Collections;
using RAIN.Core;

public class Ground : MonoBehaviour {

    private static Vector3 min, max;

    private const float LevelHeight = 0.5f;

    public static Vector3 randomLevelPosition() {
        Vector3 position = new Vector3();
        position.x = Random.Range(min.x, max.x);
        position.y = LevelHeight;
        position.z = Random.Range(min.z, max.z);
        return position;
    }

    void Start () {
        const float innerEdge = 0.9f;
        min = renderer.bounds.min * innerEdge;
        max = renderer.bounds.max * innerEdge;
    }

    void Update () {

    }
}
```

In the preceding code, we are able to ask for a random position at anytime from anywhere in the game. In the `Start` method for the `Ground` class, we store the `max` and `min` positions for it, and as we don't want positions on the very edge of the level, it is scaled to 90 percent by multiplying by `0.9f`. The `min` and `max` positions are static, so we can add a static method, `randomLevelPosition()`, that returns a random 2D position on the level with a constant height. We'll be using this method in several other spots in the code.

 We could do additional checks on this position finding to make sure that the spot never overlaps any of the walls in the scene, but to make the code simpler for this demo, we won't worry about this edge case. However, you would do this in a production game.

Reacting to game events

Next, we want to have some ships chase gold pieces, but we'll make it more dynamic than in the last demo. Create a **Sphere** object with a gold color and add a **RAIN** entity to it (by navigating to **RAIN | Create Entity**) and add a **Visual Aspect** called **Gold** to it so that AI characters can sense it. Turn this gold piece into a prefab. Instead of just placing it manually in the scene, we want them to be spawned randomly; add the code mentioned in the following screenshot to the `Ground` script:

```
7      public Transform gold;
8      private float goldTimer = 0.0f;
9      private const float goldCreateTime = 2.0f;
10
11     void Update () {
12
13         goldTimer += Time.deltaTime;
14         if(goldTimer>= goldCreateTime) {
15             Instantiate(gold, randomLevelPosition(), Quaternion.identity);
16             goldTimer = 0.0f;
17         }
18     }
```

In the Unity editor, drag the **Gold** prefab to the `Transform gold` in this script. This script randomly spawns a gold piece somewhere in the level every 2 seconds by tracking the time using `Time.deltaTime`. If you run the game now, you'll see a gold piece created randomly every 2 seconds. Next, we need ships to collect these.

Our AI ship characters will pick a random spot on the level and travel there and then after arriving, pick another random spot to go to; however, if they see a piece of gold along the way, they will stop and pick it up. To do this, create a ship object with a RAIN visual sensor with a horizontal angle of **120**, a vertical angle of **45**, and a range of **15**. The behavior tree for the ship will be straightforward. Set the root node to parallel and one **Detect** child set to look for **Gold** and store its form in the gold variable. Add another child to the root with a constraint to test if **gold == null**. If gold is not **null**, it should move to pick up the gold; if it is, pick a random spot on the level and move there. To pick a random spot in the level, create a new **Custom Action** option with a new script called ChooseRandomSpot. Set the following code for it:

```
using UnityEngine;
using System.Collections;
using System.Collections.Generic;
using RAIN.Core;
using RAIN.Action;

[RAINAction]
public class ChooseRandomSpot : RAINAction
{
    public ChooseRandomSpot()
    {
        actionName = "ChooseRandomSpot";
    }

    public override void Start(AI ai)
    {
        Vector3 moveTarget = Ground.randomLevelPosition();
        ai.WorkingMemory.SetItem("moveTarget", moveTarget);
        base.Start(ai);
    }

    public override ActionResult Execute(AI ai)
    {
        return ActionResult.SUCCESS;
    }

    public override void Stop(AI ai)
    {
        base.Stop(ai);
    }
}
```

The `Start` method uses our static `Ground` method to find a random position in the level and sets it to the `moveTarget` variable in the AI's memory. Next, add a **move** node to go to the `moveTarget` variable. If you need a review of how to set up these nodes, check *Chapter 6, Sensors and Activities*. The behavior tree for the ship should look like the following screenshot:

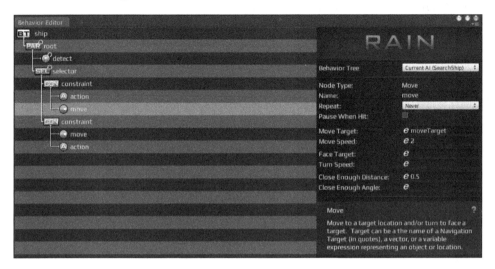

Change the ship to a prefab and add a few ships to the level. Now if you run the game, your ships will wander around, but if they see gold, they will race to pick it up and the first one there collects it.

Using RAIN's motor directly

However, if you run the game now, you'll see a problem. As expected, the ship will look for gold, and if it doesn't see any, it will pick a random position on the level and move toward it. If it sees gold along the way, it doesn't stop to pick it up; it keeps moving to its target location.

Our root node is a parallel type, so the character is always trying to detect gold, but it still ignores it while traveling. This is because our **move** node will keep running until it hits its destination, and even if it sees something, it is not interrupted until it gets there. To fix this, delete the **move** node underneath **ChooseRandomSpot Custom Action**. Then, change **ChooseRandomAction** to the code shown in the following screenshot:

```csharp
using UnityEngine;
using System.Collections;
using System.Collections.Generic;
using RAIN.Core;
using RAIN.Action;

[RAINAction]
public class ChooseRandomSpot : RAINAction
{
    public ChooseRandomSpot()
    {
        actionName = "ChooseRandomSpot";
    }

    public override void Start(AI ai)
    {
        Vector3 moveTarget = Ground.randomLevelPosition();
        ai.WorkingMemory.SetItem("moveTarget", moveTarget);
        base.Start(ai);
    }

    public override ActionResult Execute(AI ai)
    {
        GameObject gold = ai.WorkingMemory.GetItem<GameObject>("gold");
        if(gold != null) {
            return ActionResult.FAILURE;
        }

        Vector3 moveTarget = ai.WorkingMemory.GetItem<Vector3>("moveTarget");
        if(Vector3.Distance(moveTarget, ai.Body.transform.position) < 1.0f) {
            return ActionResult.SUCCESS;
        }

        ai.Motor.MoveTo(moveTarget);

        return ActionResult.RUNNING;
    }

    public override void Stop(AI ai)
    {
        base.Stop(ai);
    }
}
```

This is a big change, so let's discuss what is going on. The `Start` method is the same as before: store a random position to move to in memory. However, our action method is different. The first thing it does is it queries the memory for gold. If we have gold, we don't need to keep moving to our target, so we return failure. Then, we get our `moveTarget` variable out of memory and check the position of the `Body` variable of our AI. If it is within one unit of the goal, we say that this is close enough and return success. Finally, if we don't have gold and aren't close to `moveTarget`, we call on the AI's motor system to move to the target and keep updating it by returning the running state.

 With this update, we could have used a regular class variable to store `moveTarget`, but we keep it in memory to keep things consistent.

If you run the demo now, we will see the ships moving around as new gold appears in more expected ways, as shown in the following screenshot:

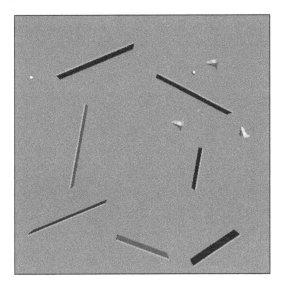

You can see the ships wandering and chasing gold in the preceding screenshot.

Adding large game events

As the last step of this demo, let's have a giant bomb go off in the scene and then have all of our AI stop to simulate having them all destroyed. To start, create a large red sphere to represent the bomb and turn it into a prefab. We will have the AI characters react to this bomb in the standard way by adding a RAIN Entity component to it and a visual aspect and have visual sensors on the ships detect it. But to show we can access the AI systems directly, let's have the bomb go off using the Ground class:

```
1  using UnityEngine;
2  using System.Collections;
3  using RAIN.Core;
4
5  public class Ground : MonoBehaviour {
6
7    ...
8      public Transform bomb;
9      public float BombTime = 30.0f;
10
11   ...
12
13     void Update () {
14
15         if(BombTime < 0.0f) {
16             return;
17         }
18
19         goldTimer += Time.deltaTime;
20         if(goldTimer >= goldCreateTime) {
21             Instantiate(gold, randomLevelPosition(), Quaternion.identity);
22             goldTimer = 0.0f;
23         }
24
25         BombTime -= Time.deltaTime;
26         if(BombTime <= 0.0f) {
27             GameObject.Instantiate(bomb);
28
29             AIRig[] AIs = GameObject.FindObjectsOfType(typeof(AIRig)) as AIRig[];
30             for(int i = 0; i < AIs.Length; i++) {
31                 AIs[i].enabled = false;
32             }
33         }
34     }
35 }
36
```

Here, we added a bomb transform to the script, so drag the bomb prefab in the Unity prefab over to it. There is also a field for a countdown that when it goes to 0, the bomb goes off and is instantiated into the scene. At this point, we grab all the AIs in the scene and send them a message, in this case, to disable it. We could have made this more complex than a simple disabling; this just shows us that we can have our game AI react to game events from anywhere. If you run the demo now, the ships stop when the bomb goes off, as shown in the following screenshot:

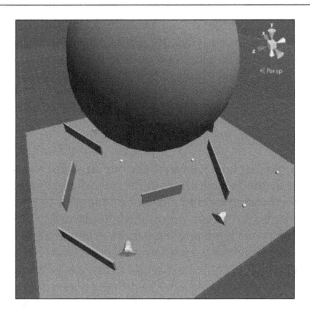

In the preceding screenshot, you can see the ships reacting to a bomb.

The React AI

We have been using RAIN for our adaption so far, but there is no reason you cannot create a demo like the one we just did with React. The basic behavior tree and node logic can stay the same. The main difference is that React doesn't use a built-in sensor system; instead, users define sensing based on what they think is the best. This can be done through Unity's built-in ray casting methods to query the scene. The following is a method adapted from React's sample that can be used with React to determine the visibility of a target. This code takes in a target and first does a simple test to see whether the target is within the field of view by finding the vector of the target from the player and comparing the angle of it and the forward direction of the AI character.

```
 7    public bool IsTargetVisible (Transform target)
 8    {
 9        Vector3 targetDirection = target.position - transform.position;
10        Ray ray = new Ray (transform.position, targetDirection);
11        varinFOV = Vector3.Angle (transform.forward, targetDirection) < 45;
12        if (inFOV) {
13            RaycastHit hit;
14            if (Physics.Raycast (ray, out hit, 1000)) {
15                return hit.collider.transform == target;
16            }
17        }
18        return false;
19    }
```

This is a simple and quick test that does a basic check, in terms of collision detection, and this is called the broad phase. Then, the Unity physics system is used to ray cast from the character to the target; this is quite expensive but a more accurate test. Using this for sensing and React's built-in behavior tree demos, like the one in this chapter, can be created.

Summary

In this chapter, we looked at how we can make our AI adapt to events in the game. This was done using methods we learned in the previous chapters, and we also took a look at RAIN's motor system to allow our adaptions to be more customizable. Our demos in this chapter have been pretty straightforward, but there is no reason why this demo couldn't be extended to have more events to send and more reactions defined in the character behavior trees. However, our demos have been missing one important thing, which is yet to be discussed: the player. In the next chapter, we will discuss how AI characters attack by adding a player to our scene and having our characters react and attack. We will discuss how to create enemies for the player and have them attack the player.

8
Attacking

Fighting is an important part of a game's AI. For many games, fighting with the player is the main game mechanic and the most noticeable AI in the game. We will discuss the common methods for attack AI, how to make an enemy character chase and attack the player, and then have the enemy character take cover and hide from the player.

In this chapter, you will learn about:

- Designing attack AI in RAIN 2.1.4
- Creating basic chase attack AI
- Creating and covering attack AI
- Having AI attack in groups

An overview of attack AI

Attack AI is a large and much studied subject. When you start dealing with things such as different attack moves based on different player actions or having enemies coordinate attacks, the AI can become quite complex. However, designing good AI that attacks is the same as designing for other AI scenarios we have looked at so far in this book. First, we need sensors for our AI characters to perceive game events and to create aspects in the game world, tagging what they can sense. Then, we define behavior trees for the characters, directing them to change actions based on sensor response or other game states, such as running out of ammo. Defining different behaviors is the main part of setting up attack AI.

We'll look at two foundational AI attack behaviors in our demos in this chapter. The first will use multiple sensors on the AI to determine when to chase and when to stop and attack. The second behavior we will look at is the duck and cover type, where the enemy attacker will retreat to a safe position after attacking, and this is based on set navigation points. These are both best illustrated through demos, so let's start one now.

The attack demo

Like our previous demos, we will start with a basic scene with a ground and walls. The demos here will involve an enemy ship attacking a player, so add a ship to the scene, name it `player`, and add simple controls to move the ship around. Also, tint the color of the material to make the player ship stand out from the enemy ship that we'll add in a moment. Of course, the player ship isn't an AI, so it doesn't need a RAIN AIRig, but it does need to have a RAIN Entity component. With the player selected, go to **RAIN | Create Entity**. Next, it needs a visual aspect for the AI enemies to see it; from the **Add Aspect** dropdown, select **Visual Aspect** and rename the aspect to `player`. This provides a base for our attack demo. This is how the RAIN attack demos will look with a player ship:

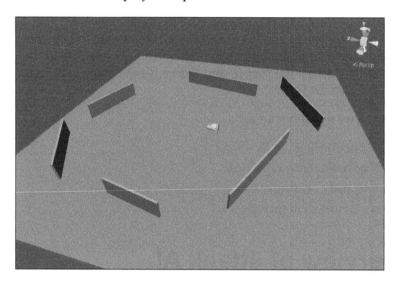

Next, we need an enemy for the attack. The enemies will also be ship models, and as we are focusing on just the AI, we won't worry about the actual game mechanics of attacking, such as having the ship fire projectiles at the player, then having the player respond to being hit, and so on. Usually, these kind of attack AI states involve playing different animations for the AI, and we will explore these more in *Chapter 10, Animation and AI*; for now, we just need a simple visualization to illustrate the attack. To visualize, we'll store a Boolean variable in RAIN's working memory flagging if the enemy is attacking and if so, start blinking.

To set this up, add a ship to the scene and add an AIRig to it by going to **RAIN | Create AI**. To add an attack flag, select the RAIN **Memory** tab on the ship AI (the light bulb icon) and from **Add Variable**, select **bool**. Rename the variable to `isAttacking` and leave it to the default value of false. The memory with the `isAttacking` variable set should look like the following screenshot:

To use this variable, create a new script called `Enemy.cs` and add it to the enemy ship. Change the code to the following:

```
1   using UnityEngine;
2   using System.Collections;
3   using RAIN.Core;
4
5   public class Enemy : MonoBehaviour {
6
7       float blinkTime = 0.0f;
8       const float blinkLength = 0.1f;
9
10      AIRig aiRig = null;
11
12      void Start () {
13          aiRig = GetComponentInChildren<AIRig>();
14      }
15
16      void Update () {
17
18          bool isAttacking = aiRig.AI.WorkingMemory.GetItem<bool>("isAttacking");
19
20          if(!isAttacking) {
21              gameObject.renderer.material.color = Color.white;
22              return;
23          }
24
25          blinkTime += Time.deltaTime;
26          if(blinkTime > blinkLength) {
27              blinkTime = -blinkLength;
28          }
29
30          gameObject.renderer.material.color = blinkTime < 0.0f ? Color.green : Color.white;
31      }
32  }
33
```

Here, we store the AIRig for the entity by retrieving it at the start. Then, we get the `isAttacking` variable from the working memory, and if the enemy is attacking, the ship starts blinking green. If it's not attacking, the ship stays its default color, which is white. Create a new prefab in Unity named `Enemy` and drag the ship into it. Now we have enemies that can start attacking the player, and we can start setting up our AI.

The chase and attack demo

In the first demo, we will build an enemy ship that senses for the player, and if it sees the player, it starts moving toward it and then attacks it. A simple version of this would be to have the enemy wander with a visual sensor to detect the player, and if it sees the player, the enemy will move toward it and attack it. This would work but it really wouldn't be any different from the demo from *Chapter 7, Adaptation*, where the ship had to search for and collect gold. To make it a little different, we'll use a two-sensor approach. We will have one larger sensor on the enemy that detects the player, and if the enemy senses the player aspect, it will start chasing the player. Then, there is a second smaller sensor that attacks the player, that is, if it senses the player, then the enemy stops chasing and it instead attacks. This gives the effect of chasing the player but when the enemy gets closer, it stops and starts attacking, instead of just chasing and attacking at the same time.

To begin setting these up, go to the **Perception** tab on the enemy AI rig (the little eye icon tab) and add a visual sensor called `ChaseSensor`. This should be pretty large and cover most of the scene. Then, add a second visual sensor and call it `AttackSensor`. Make this one about a third the size of `ChaseSensor`. The setup should look something like the following screenshot:

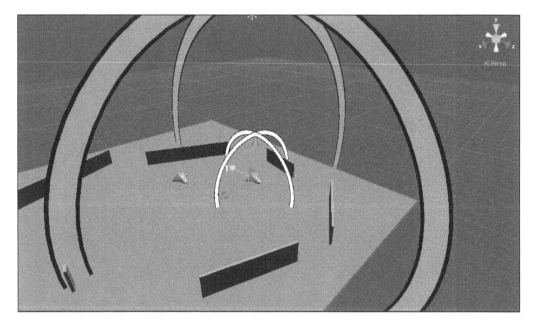

The preceding screenshot shows our enemy setup with two sensors: one will be used to chase and the smaller one will be used to attack.

 Using multiple sensors of the same type is a powerful tool to have AI characters react to things differently based on how far away they are.

Now we have our sensor, we can work on the behavior tree for the enemy. Select the **Mind** tab of the enemy AI rig and open the behavior editor. Create a new behavior tree called **ChaseAndAttack**. The enemy will detect and chase or attack the player at the same time, so right-click on the **root** node and change its type to **Parallel**. Then, add two detect nodes, one for the chase sensor and one for the attack sensor. For the chase detect node, set **Sensor** to **"ChaseSensor"**, **Aspect** to **"player"**, and the form variable to playerChase (remember to watch out for the quotes). For the attack sensor, set **Sensor** to **"AttackSensor"**, **Aspect** also to **"player"**, and the form variable to playerAttack. Then, add a constraint node, which will go off if either of the sensors has found something, so set its constraint to **playerChase != null ||** **playerAttack != null**. Then, add a **selector** node under the **constraint** node that will handle the attack and chase logic. The multiple visual sensors behavior tree should look like the following screenshot:

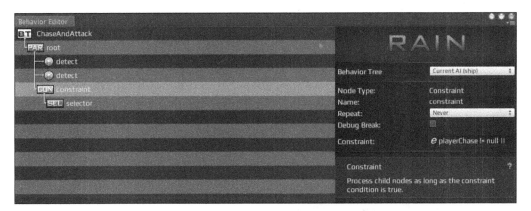

Remember the **selector** node will continue to run its children until one succeeds, so first we will check for attack. If playerAttack has a value (that is, it is not null), we will set isAttacking to true, and if not, set it to false. Add a **constraint** node under the **selector** that checks for attacks and set its constraint to **playerAttack != null**. As the playerAttack variable is not null, add an **expression** node to start attacking with an expression value of isAttacking, which is equal to true.

Then, if `playerAttack` is null, we want the attack to stop, so add another expression with `isAttacking`, which is equal to false. The attack setup on our enemy behavior tree should look like the following screenshot:

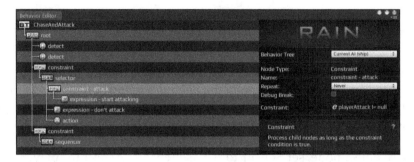

If you run the demo now, when the player gets sensed by `AttackSensor`, the enemy will start attacking and stop when the player is out of range.

 Our attack behavior here is very simple; we are just flashing the ship. However, there's no reason why you couldn't add additional attack nodes and states to make the behavior more realistic.

Finally, we need to have the enemy chase the player if it is not attacking, so add a custom node called `Chase` to the bottom of the selector. Create a `Chase` script for it and set the `Chase` code to the following:

```
using UnityEngine;
using System.Collections;
using System.Collections.Generic;
using RAIN.Core;
using RAIN.Action;

[RAINAction]
public class Chase : RAINAction
{
    public GameObject player;

    public override void Start(AI ai)
    {
        base.Start(ai);

        player = GameObject.Find("player");
    }

    public override ActionResult Execute(AI ai)
    {
        if(player == null) {
            return ActionResult.FAILURE;
        }

        ai.Motor.MoveTo(player.transform.position);

        return ActionResult.RUNNING;
    }

    public override void Stop(AI ai)
    {
        base.Stop(ai);
    }
}
```

This code first finds the `player` GameObject and then just moves to the player's position. This is unlike the code in the demos in *Chapter 7, Adaptation*, where we did a check to stop moving if the character gets very close to the moving target. When the character gets close to the target, it will stop moving and start attacking, so we don't need checks. If you run the demo now, the enemy will chase the player and start attacking:

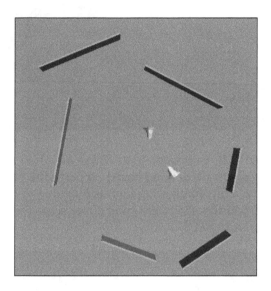

The preceding screenshot shows how an enemy attacking the player will look at the end.

Creating cover AI

Our AI enemy will just keep attacking the player as long as it is close enough to the ship. However, this isn't very realistic; we'd like the enemy ship to attack for a little bit but then duck and head for cover. We could have this hiding behavior be based on a response to the player fighting back, but for this demo, we will make it a constant value of 5 seconds; after attacking the player for 5 seconds, it will hide.

To set this up, first we'll add an `isHidingbool` variable to our behavior tree that is set to true after 5 seconds of attacking. Create a new **constraint** node under the **root** parallel node with the **playerAttack != null && isHiding == false** expression. This node's children start when `playerAttack` is valid and we are not already hiding from the player. Add a **sequencer** node under this constraint so it will go through all of its children. The first child needs to be a new timer node with the **Seconds** value of **5** and **Returns** set to **Success**. Next, copy the **don't attack** node and add it below the timer so that the enemy won't attack as it's running to hide.

Then, add another **expression** node to set isHiding to true; its expression value should be **isHiding = true**. The behavior tree should be like the following screenshot:

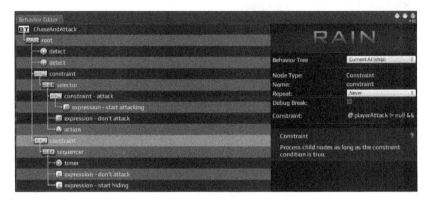

Finally, we need to have hiding spots to go to. These are often predefined; in shooting games, hiding spots are defined based on paths the player is expected to take. To do this, create a few navigation targets by going to **RAIN | Create Navigation Target** and add them to some good cover spots for the enemy. Here's how they can be arranged:

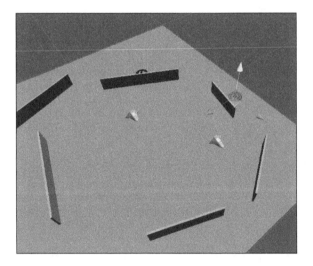

This is how we set up navigation targets for hiding spots.

Next, we need to have the AI choose a point to take cover. Lastly, we need to select and move to a hiding spot. To organize the tree better, add a **selector** node above the hiding **constraint** node. Then, add another **constraint** node below the **selector** node and create a custom action node with a new ChooseHidingSpot class.

The tree should look like the following screenshot:

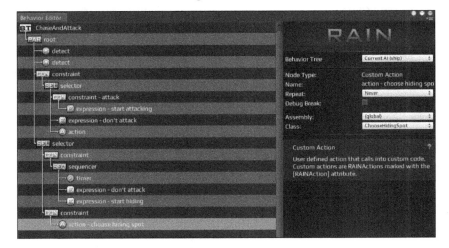

 When creating larger trees, giving the nodes descriptive names helps keep the tree organized and easy to understand.

The following is the code for our action to choose a hiding spot:

```
8    [RAINAction]
9    public class ChooseHidingSpot : RAINAction
10   {
11       Vector3 hideTarget;
12
13       public override void Start(AI ai)
14       {
15           NavigationTargetRig[] coverPoints = GameObject.FindObjectsOfType(typeof(NavigationTargetRig)) as NavigationTargetRig[];
16
17           if(coverPoints.Length == 0)
18           {
19               return;
20           }
21
22           float length = float.MaxValue;
23           Vector3 target = Vector3.zero;
24           foreach(NavigationTargetRig obj in coverPoints)
25           {
26               if(Vector3.Distance(ai.Body.transform.position, obj.Target.PositionOffset) < length)
27               {
28                   target = obj.Target.PositionOffset;
29               }
30           }
31
32           hideTarget = target;
33
34           base.Start(ai);
35       }
36
37       public override ActionResult Execute(AI ai)
38       {
39           if(Vector3.Distance(hideTarget, ai.Body.transform.position) < 1.0f) {
40               return ActionResult.SUCCESS;
41           }
42
43           ai.Motor.MoveTo(hideTarget);
44
45           return ActionResult.RUNNING;
46       }
47
48       public override void Stop(AI ai)
49       {
50           base.Stop(ai);
51       }
52   }
```

Here, when we start the action, we find all the `NavigationTargetRig` objects and store them in the `coverPoints` array. Then, we go through each target and find the one closest to the enemy. Once we have the closest target, we store it in `hideTarget` and start moving to it.

As an addition to this, we can have the enemy start attacking again after hiding. Add the following line right before `ActionResult.SUCCESS` is returned:

```
ai.WorkingMemory.SetItem("isHiding", false);
```

This just updates the memory to set the hiding value to false and the attack will restart. This is a simple extension and the attack can be easily extended to better attack behaviors.

Group attacks

We spent *Chapter 4*, *Crowd Chaos*, and *Chapter 5*, *Crowd Control*, looking at group behaviors, and we won't go through a full demo of attacking in groups here, but we should discuss a few main points. With the demo in this chapter, we can add more ships and they will attack in a fairly believable manner. However, there are ways to make it better by considering other enemy positions.

When the enemy ships choose a cover position, a simple method for a group is to track each position if an enemy is already there. Then, when selecting a cover position, each enemy won't go to one that is occupied, making the enemies more diverse in their attacks.

Similarly, when attacking the player, instead of just going as close as possible, the attack pattern can be coordinated. Instead of just going directly to the player, a set of points can be defined radially around the player, so enemies surround and attack it. The key to these group behaviors is enemies taking into account the behavior of other enemies.

Summary

In this chapter, we looked at attack AI, focusing on how to have enemies chase and attack a player and then how to evade. These are basic attack behaviors and can be extended to more complex and game-specific behaviors, and we discussed how to do this when creating groups of enemies.

In the next chapter, we will look at another special AI case, which is driving and cars. However, instead of using a general-purpose AI system such as RAIN or React AI, we will use an AI plugin specifically designed for cars that takes into account physics to create realistic driving.

9
Driving

In this chapter, we will look at another specialized AI, driving. The other AI we have looked at so far had pretty simple movement for characters. However, car movement needs to take into account physics, and this makes driving AI more complex, which is why we need an AI system specially designed for driving. The AI driving system we will use for our demos is Smart Car AI. Smart Car uses Unity's built-in navigation mesh system, so we will also take a look at it.

In this chapter, you will learn about:

- Setting up the AI driving system
- Creating a Unity navigation mesh
- Using Smart Car to drive AI along a path
- Using Smart Car to drive and avoid obstacles

An overview of driving

When designing AI for our characters, one of the basic concepts is to have AI move with the same rules as the player. If you ever played any old racing games, sometimes the opponent cars wouldn't follow the same physics as the player, zooming along unrealistically and therefore creating a bad player experience. So, it's important to take car physics into account, including the shape of the car and four wheels, and have the AI move in the same way as the player. This is the main reason for using an AI system especially designed for autos and driving, instead of a general-purpose game AI system we have been using such as RAIN.

The driving system we'll use is Smart Car AI by BoneBreaker, which at the time of writing this book is available in Unity Asset Store for $10. It takes into account physics for the car and uses ray casting to sense the car's environment. It actually uses two systems for navigation, which are Unity's built-in navigation system to determine paths along a road and ray casting to sense obstacles and make adjustments to the car.

Additionally, Smart Car uses four-wheel physics for realistic movement. Because of the advanced use of physics, we can't just drop any car model in and have it work automatically; we will need to configure Smart Car to use the model's wheel colliders. Wheel colliders are a type of Unity's physics colliders that are specifically made for vehicles. Let's look at how to set up a car.

Setting up a Smart Car vehicle

As Smart Car uses a realistic car setup, there are many options to configure your vehicle. To create a Smart Car vehicle, you'll need a car model with different models for wheels and Unity wheel colliders setup on them. After adding a car model to your scene, import the Smart Car 2.3 package and attach the `SmartAICar2_3.cs` script from `SmartAICar2.3/Scripts`. In the following screenshot, you can see some of the Smart Car AI fields from the script:

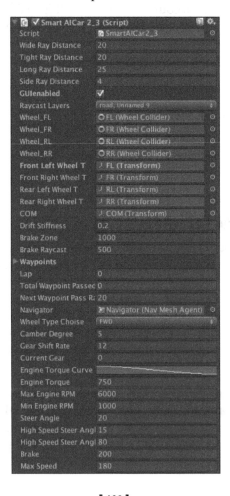

There are fields here you can customize such as Engine properties, including **Engine Torque Curve**, and the distances for the ray casts used for sensing. Most of these can be left to default values, but to run the script, you'll need to fill in the wheel properties, dragging from your model the colliders for the four wheels to the **Wheel_FL**, **Wheel_FR**, **Wheel_RL**, and **Wheel_RR** properties. You also need transforms for the wheel set. Also, there needs to be a transform for **center of mass** (**COM**), a lower point in the middle of the car. If COM is placed in the wrong position, the physics of the car can be very unexpected. If you fill these out, the car is set up but it still won't run in a game as it still needs waypoints and a Unity navigation mesh setup, which we will add in the demo.

The Smart Car AI demo

Now, we'll start setting up our driving demo that will have a car driving along a road and avoiding obstacles.

Setting up a Unity test scene

Besides needing Smart Car, we'll need an environment for our AI cars to drive in. We'll use Car Tutorial v1.3 that is made by Unity, which you can download for free from the Asset Store. Import the project and open **TheTrack** scene from the imported Scenes folder. Next, add a car to the scene. The car prefab that comes with Car Tutorial doesn't have the complete wheel physics setup, so you can configure it using the steps in the last section or use the **EnemyAICar** prefab from Smart Car. To make the car work better with the **Tutorial** scene, extend the rays a little, set **Wide** and **Tight Ray Distance** both to 40 and **Long Ray Distance** to 50. This keeps the car from hitting obstacles when going too fast and missing tight turns. Once you have a car in the scene configured for Smart Car, select the **Main_Camera** object and set your car to **Target** for the **Car Camera** script.

If you start the demo now, the car still won't run but the main camera in the scene will follow it:

This screenshot is of the **Main_Camera** game object of Car Tutorial. These are the settings for the **TheTrack** scene with **Target** set to the Smart Car prefab.

Another setting in the scene that can cause problems is the `TunnelSoundTrigger` Sound Toggler script. As it isn't important to use, select the `TunnelSoundTrigger` script and remove that component to avoid errors later.

Using Unity's built-in NavMesh system

The next thing we need for our car demo is a navigation mesh. Smart Car uses Unity's built-in system. Unity's system is similar to RAIN's but we haven't used it much yet as unlike other plugins, Unity does not have a built-in behavior tree system. Fortunately, we don't need behavior trees for our car demos, so navigate to **Window | Navigation**.

This brings up the **Navigation** tab with three subtabs to help configure the NavMesh:

- **Object**: This helps you filter what objects in the scene are part of the navigation mesh. Any objects that are tagged with **Navigation Static** will be included in the mesh as a walkable area.

- **Bake**: This has options to bake the mesh. The two most important options are **Radius** and **Height**, which are dimensions for the character to navigate on the mesh.

- **Layers**: This allows you to customize the placement of different navigation meshes on different layers.

For our demo, we want only the roads to be navigable. Select the other building and miscellaneous objects in the scene and set their static property (which is to the right of their name in **Inspector**) to not have **Navigation Static** set. Then, for the different road objects, such as **Road_Coll**, **Road_Coll01**, and so on, make sure that they have **Navigation Static** checked. Then, go back to the **Navigation** tab and click on **Bake**. If you have everything set correctly after you bake, you should see the navigation mesh in the same area as the road:

This is how the road navigation mesh setup should look.

This should have been pretty quick to recreate, but depending on the character size settings and the amount of geometry in the scene, this can take a bit of time. We will discuss navigation meshes more and the algorithm behind how they are generated in *Chapter 11, Advanced NavMesh Generation*.

> **NavMeshAgent** is the built-in Unity component to create characters that move on a navigation mesh. Smart Car uses this internally. We won't be using this class directly but you can if you want to try more of Unity's built-in navigation system; it is a good class to look at.

Setting up waypoints

The final step to get a car driving is to set up waypoints for the car to follow. The NavMesh we created defines the area that the car can navigate to and the waypoints define the general path the car should follow. Create a new empty game object and name it Road Waypoints. Then, create a few more empties with the names **waypoint 1**, **waypoint 2**, **waypoint 3**, and so on. Place the waypoint empties at different parts along the road. Note that the NavMesh for the road will define how to get from one waypoint to the next, so the line between waypoints doesn't have to go through the road. For instance, you could have one waypoint at the start of a curve and the second at the end and the car would still go around the curve through the waypoints. In the Smart AICar script, set the empties to the **Waypoints** field. After doing this, the waypoints will be visualized in the edit or view to make adjusting their locations easier. Refer to the following screenshot, and you can see how the visualization of Smart car AI waypoints looks:

If you run the demo after setting the waypoints, the car drives realistically across the road. If you want to fine-tune the car more, remember there are many physics settings with Smart Car that can be adjusted to change how the car acts.

Adding obstacles to driving

As Smart Car uses a combination of a NavMesh and ray casting, you can add objects dynamically to the scene, and as long as they have colliders attached (and are on a car's **Recast Layers**), the car will avoid them. To try this out, add a few large cylinders to the road, as shown in the following screenshot:

Then, in the **Recast Layers** dropdown for your car, make sure that it is set to ray cast on the same layer as the obstacles. Select a **Cylinder** object and in **Inspector**, select **Add Layer**. We need to create an obstacles layer, so select the dropdown and in the first slot for **User Layer**, set it to **obstacles**.

Then, for each cylinder, set its layer to **obstacles**:

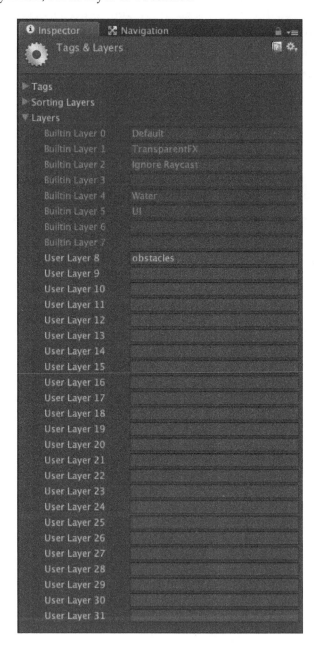

This is how the **Inspector** window should look after creating the obstacle layer.

Then, for Smart Car in the **Raycast Layers** dropdown, make sure that the **obstacles** layer is selected. Once you have this set up, if you run the demo, the car will drive and avoid the obstacles. The car still uses physics for its control, and sometimes if you place the obstacles too close to one another, the car will run into one. Fortunately, in this case, the car will back up and then drive past it, which is a nice touch Smart Car has.

The cylinders are static objects in our scene, but as ray casting is used, there is no reason why you cannot script dynamic objects and the car will still avoid them. To see this, run the demo and in the scene view, grab one of the obstacles and move it around to block the car; the car will try to avoid it.

Additional features

We've just completed creating a driving demo with a car avoiding obstacles, but there are a few more things you can do with driving AI. We can add brake and drift zones to help configure the general behavior of the car as it drives around the scene, and we can integrate Smart Car with other AI systems such as RAIN.

Adding brake zones and drift zones

Another interesting thing you can do with Smart Car is define zones in the level to either cause the car to brake and slow down or adjust the friction of the car to make it drift. These are similar to the vector fields we saw in *Chapter 5*, *Crowd Control*, where we place them in the level to affect the AI, and they aren't visible to the player but are good to use for scripting level experiences. To create a brake or drift zone in your game, add a cube to the game (go to **GameObject | Create Other | Cube**) and scale and translate the area you want to tag in the level. In the Inspector window for the cube, set its tag to **BrakeZone** and for a drift zone set the tag to **DriftZone**. Next, in **Box Collider** for the cube, check **Is Trigger** to true, so the car will get a message of intersecting with a cube but won't stop and collide with it. Lastly, in the **Inspector** window, uncheck **Mesh Renderer** so that the cube is invisible in the game. Now when you run the demo, if the car's speed is **25** or over when it enters the brake zone, you will see it slow down, and if its speed is **15** or over, you will see it drift in the drift zone.

Integrating with other AI systems

In this demo, we've seen that setting up an AI car that drives around is easy to do with Smart Car. However, what if your game isn't just a driving game but has car driving as one part of the game? If that's the case, you can mix Smart Car with another AI system easily. For RAIN integration, import the RAIN package into your scene. Then, go to **RAIN | Create Entity** and then select **Add Aspect: Visual Aspects**. This creates an entity with an aspect that can be sensed by additional RAIN AI entities you can create in the scene, making the car just one part of a larger AI system.

Summary

In this chapter, we looked at Smart Car, an AI system specifically for car AI. We discussed why automotive AI is different than most AIs because of the physics involved, and we also saw how to set up a car model, create a path for the car, and add obstacles. We also looked at using Unity's built-in navigation mesh system, instead of using third-party ones such as RAIN, and discussed additional features for car AI and how we can integrate it with another AI system such as RAIN.

In the next two chapters, we will look at how to combine character animations and AI to give them a realistic appearance and learn more about creating complex navigation meshes for different AIs.

10
Animation and AI

Part of having realistic game AI is having characters play animations at times appropriate to the AI character's state. In this chapter, we will look at animation and how it is integrated with RAIN, both with Unity's legacy animation system and Mecanim.

In this chapter, you will learn about the following:

- Why animation management is an important part of game AI
- Managing animation with behavior trees and Unity's legacy animation
- Managing animation by AI with Unity's Mecanim animation system

An overview of animation

When you think about game AI, first you probably think about things such as creating virtual minds and making characters "think". When I first started learning about game AI years ago, I didn't think animation was really important for game AI since it wasn't part of creating a virtual mind. But then I attended some AI sessions at the Game Developers Conference and found out that one of the most discussed topics in AI was integrating AI with animation systems; this is when I realized it really is an important part of game AI. This makes sense since game AI is about modeling real thinking instead of focusing on giving characters the appearance of thinking, so having the characters play animations that match their state is important. We can think of animations as just a visual depiction of the current state of the character.

The method we'll look at for integrating animations with the AI is RAIN's animation integration with Unity. RAIN has an **Animation** tab (with an icon of a running man) in its AIRig. In this tab, animation clips can be configured using one of two RAIN animators.

RAIN has a **BasicAnimator** option to configure clips with Unity's legacy animation and a **MecaninAnimator** option used to set up Mecanim animations. Once these animations are set up, RAIN has an animate node in its behavior tree system that can be used to call different animation states. Usually, this is done in conjunction with a parallel node with the animate node being one of its children. This way the animation can run at the same time as the other logic is being executed in the tree.

The best way to see this is through demos. For these, we need to have two characters: a legacy and a Mecanim setup. To do this, our demo project will use two demos that are made by Unity and can be downloaded for free from the Asset Store. The first is **Penelope Complete Project v1.1**. This contains the Penelope character we will use for the Unity legacy demo. The other project is **Mecanim Example Scenes v1.0** that will be for the Mecanim setup character, Teddy. Create a new project and import both of these and the latest RAIN package. Once these are set up, we can start building the animation demo.

The AI animation demo

As the first step, create a new scene and add a plane to it with a scale of X equal to 10, Y equal to 1, and Z equal to 10 to give us a floor where characters can walk around (and if you want, change its material so it's not white). Then, add the **penelope** model to your scene that's at `Assets/Objects/penelopeFX`. Next, we'll do our basic RAIN setup and add a navigation mesh by going to **RAIN | Create NavMesh**. Make sure the navigation mesh will cover the floor, so change its **Size** to **100** and then generate the mesh. Next, create a waypoint route by going to **RAIN | Create Waypoint Route**, rename it `PenelopeRoute`, and add a few points in front of the **penelope** model for the character to walk. Lastly, add a RAIN AI object by selecting **penelope** and going to **RAIN | Create AI**. Your screen should look similar to the following screenshot:

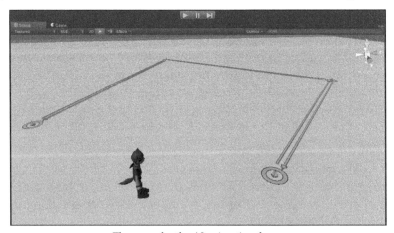

The scene for the AI animation demo

If you need more details on how to set up a scene with a character patrolling a path, refer to *Chapter 2, Patrolling*.

Now that we have a scene, let's create a behavior tree for Penelope; we want her to just walk following the path and stopping at the end. Select Penelope's AI object and open **Behavior Editor**. Create a new behavior tree called `WalkPenelope` and add a patrol route node to the root. Set the route to **"PenelopeRoute"**. We just want Penelope to walk the route once and then stop, so set the **Repeat** field to **Never** and the **Loop Type** field to **One Way**. Lastly, set the **Move Target Variable** field to **moveTarget** and create a child **move** node that uses **moveTarget** to move. The tree should look like the following screenshot:

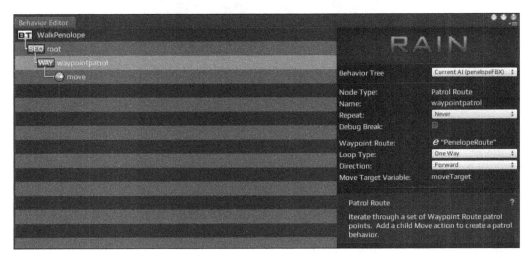

If you run the demo now, Penelope will travel around the path, but there will be no character animation; she will just slide on the ground. To fix this, we'll add animation to our character.

Configuring RAIN animations

To configure animation for Penelope on her RAIN menu, select the **Animation** tab. (Again, this is the tab with a little figure running on it.) RAIN supports two animation systems: **BasicAnimator** and **MecanimAnimator**. Since the Penelope character doesn't use Mecanim, leave the animator as basic. The **Add Animation State** dropdown will then be automatically populated with the different animation clips available. Choose the animation states **run** and **idle**.

Your animation tab should look like the following screenshot:

Here are some of the animation parameters:

- **State Name**: This specifies the name of the animation clip; this is what we'll use in the animate node in the behavior tree when calling animations.

- **Animation Clip**: This specifies the legacy animation clip associated with this state.

- **Fade in Time, Fade Out Time**: This specifies the amount of time required to fade in and out of the animation. This can be useful to create smooth transitions between animation clips.

- **Wrap Mode**: This provides the wrap mode for the animation. This can be left to default to use the clip's default settings. Other options are to loop or to play the animation once and go to the beginning or end of the clip.

Using the animate node

Now we need to configure the behavior tree to play the animations. As our first step, let's get Penelope running. Right-click on the **root** node in the `WalkPenelope` behavior tree and go to **Switch To Parallel** and then rename the node to `parallel`. By being parallel, we can add an animate node and have it update the animation at the same time as the patrol node is being executed. So add an animate node, rename it to `animate run`, and set **Animation State** to **run**. Your setting should look like the following screenshot:

If you run the demo now, you'll see the Penelope character perform the animation while it's moving. But the timing seems a little off. Change the moving speed of the **move** node to **3**. Then slow down the animation a little by going back to the **Animation** tab and setting the **Speed** field to **0.75**. If you run the demo now, the animation is a bit better. But when Penelope gets to the end of the route, the run animation just keeps on playing. To fix this, let's track a variable in the memory called `stopped`. When it is false, the run animation will play as it does now, and when `stopped` is `true`, an idle animation will be played instead.

The first thing you need to do to fix the animation's issues with ending is add a **selector** node as the new root. Remember, the **selector** node is used for the `if/else` logic, so we'll use it to switch between its running state and playing an idle animation. Add a **constraint** node under **selector** and rename it to `is stopped`. Set **Constraint** to **stopped == false**. Then add a new animate node under the **selector** node, name it `animate idle`, and set **Animation State** to **idle**. This will only start running when `stopped` is true, so we need to add an expression node to run the **expression** node after our moving is done. Make a new **sequencer** node and make it the parent of **waypointpatrol**. Then add an expression node under the **sequencer** node with an **Expression** value of **stopped = true**.

This should look like the following screenshot:

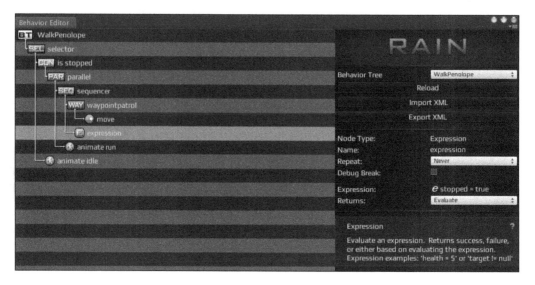

To summarize, the selector acts as `if/else` using the `stopped` variable in the memory, which is automatically created in the tree when we start using it. Then the run animation is played in parallel while the character is moving, and when the moving is done, the expression sets **stopped = true** and the idle animation is played. If you run the animation now, Penelope will run and then switch to idle at the end of the path.

However, there is one problem: the transition from the running to the idle state is very abrupt. If you run the demo, you'll easily notice a visual jump from the running to the idle state for Penelope at the end of the path. To help with this, you can adjust the ramping parameters for the animations. Go back to RAIN's **Animation** tab and set the **Fade Out Time** field of the run animation to **2**. Now, if you run the animation, Penelope will start to transition out of the running state for two seconds, and although everything doesn't look perfect, the transition is much smoother than before. Feel free to play with other ramp settings to get a better effect.

This shows how RAIN works with Unity's legacy animation system; now, let's look at Mecanim.

RAIN and the Mecanim demo

Mecanim is Unity's latest animation system that's able to play animations on arbitrary characters. We won't go into detail on how Mecanim works and instead focus just on RAIN's usage.

For this demo, we will use a character already set up for Mecanim from Unity's sample. If you haven't already done so, download and import Unity's Mecanim demo, **Mecanim Example Scenes v1.0**, which is free on the Asset Store. Add the teddy bear character from `Character/Teddy2/TeddyBar.fbx` to your scene. Then, in the **Animator** component for Teddy, set the **Controller** field to **IdleRunJump** from **Controllers**. Then, add a RAIN AIRig to Teddy by going to **RAIN | Create AI**. We'll have Teddy walk on a different route, so create a new waypoint patrol route and name it `TeddyRoute`. Your scene should look like this:

In the preceding screenshot, you can see Teddy with a new path set up in your scene.

Next, we need to configure animations for Teddy. Go to the **Animation** tab in Teddy's RAIN AIRig and select **MecanimAnimator**. Then, we need to add states for running and idling. Select **Base Layer.Run** and **Base Layer.Idle** from **Add Animation State**.

Your screen should look like the following:

These are the basic animations added to Teddy. Besides adding the states, we need to set Mecanim parameters. From the teddy bear object's **Animator** component, open **Controller** for **IdleRunJump**. The following is the Teddy Mecanim diagram:

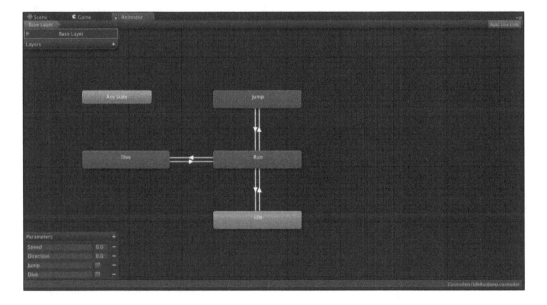

This shows the different parameters for the Teddy character; we'll only be setting **Speed**. Go back to the **Animation** tab for Teddy to set up **Start Parameter** under **Base Layer.Run**. Set the **Parameter Name** field to **Speed** and leave the **Parameter Type** field to **Float** and the **Parameter Value** field to **1**. Then, do the same for **Base Layer.Idle**, except set the **Parameter Value** field to **0**. The new settings should look like this:

This sets up the animation. Now we can set up the behavior tree for Teddy. Create a new behavior tree called **WalkTeddy** and recreate the behavior tree from **WalkPenelope**.

 With RAIN, you can copy and paste nodes from one part of a tree to another and from one tree to a different one.

From the animate node's perspective, it doesn't matter whether the animator is Mecanim or not, so we only need to make a few simple changes. Change the waypoint patrol node's waypoint route to **"TeddyRoute"**. Then, in the **animate run** node, set **Animation State** to **Base Layer.Run** and set animation idle's **Animation State** field to **Base Layer.Idle**. And one important change for Mecanim is to set the animate node's **Repeat** field to **Forever**. The following screenshot shows the new behavior tree:

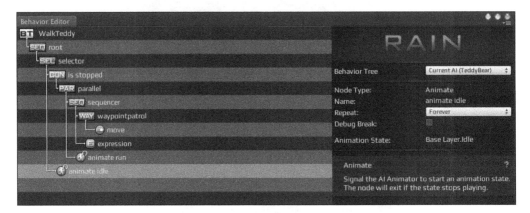

If you run the demo now, you'll see Teddy running along the path and then be in the idle state at the end, just like Penelope. But there is one problem: Teddy is running way too fast. The reason is that RAIN is moving the model and the animation system is also applying movement to the character, making Teddy move fast artificially. To fix this, go back to the **Animator** component of **Teddy** and uncheck **Apply Root Motion**. This will keep the animation system from applying movement and Teddy will now run at a better rate. Running the demo now, Teddy will run and idle at the end.

Additional Mecanim nodes

Besides using the animate node for Mecanim, RAIN has additional nodes specifically for Mecanim, mostly useful in special cases. The nodes are as follows:

- **Mecanim IK**: This node is used to modify the inverse kinematics on part of a model
- **Mecanim State**: This node is used to check the animation controller state
- **Mecanim Parameter**: This node is used to change a Mecanim parameter

These are less-used nodes but are good to know.

Summary

In this chapter, we looked at how to integrate animation with our AI. We saw how to use RAIN's animate node to change the character animation from its behavior tree with both Unity's legacy animation system and Mecanim. In the next chapter, we will go back to discussing character movement across a scene. We will look at more advanced uses of navigation meshes and how to create them in more detail to give our characters better movement.

11
Advanced NavMesh Generation

Navigation mesh generation is one of the most important topics in game AI. We have been using navigation meshes in almost all the chapters in this book, but haven't looked at them in detail. In this chapter, we will provide a more detailed overview of navigation meshes and look at the algorithm used to generate them. Then, we'll look at different options of customizing our navigation meshes better.

In this chapter, you will learn about:

- The working of navigation mesh generation and the algorithm behind it
- Advanced options for customizing navigation meshes
- Creating advanced navigation meshes with RAIN

An overview of a NavMesh

To use navigation meshes effectively, also referred to as **NavMeshes**, the first things we need to know are what exactly navigation meshes are and how they are created. A navigation mesh is a definition of the area an AI character can travel to in a level. It is a mesh, but it is not intended to be rendered or seen by the player; instead, it is used by the AI system. A NavMesh usually does not cover all the area in a level (if it did, we wouldn't need one) as it's just the area a character can walk. The mesh is also almost always a simplified version of the geometry. For instance, you could have a cave floor in a game with thousands of polygons along the bottom that show different details in the rock; however, for the navigation mesh, the areas would just be a handful of very large polygons that give a simplified view of the level. The purpose of a navigation mesh is to provide this simplified representation to the rest of the AI system as a way to find a path between two points on a level for a character. This is its purpose; let's discuss how they are created.

It used to be a common practice in the games industry to create navigation meshes manually. A designer or artist would take the completed level geometry and create one using standard polygon mesh modeling tools and save it. As you might imagine, this allowed for nice, custom, efficient meshes, was also a time sink, as every time the level changed, the navigation mesh would need to be manually edited and updated. In recent years, there has been more research in automatic navigation mesh generation.

There are many approaches to automatic navigation mesh generation, but the most popular is **Recast**, originally developed and designed by Mikko Monomen. Recast takes in level geometry and a set of parameters that define the character, such as the size of the character and how big of steps it can take, and then does a multipass approach to filter and creates the final NavMesh. The most important phase of this is **voxelizing** the level based on an inputted cell size. This means the level geometry is divided into voxels (cubes), creating a version of the level geometry where everything is partitioned into different boxes called cells. Then, the geometry in each of these cells is analyzed and simplified based on its intersection with the sides of the boxes and is culled based on things such as the slope of the geometry or how big a step height is between geometry. This simplified geometry is then merged and triangulated to make a final navigation mesh that can be used by the AI system.

> The source code and more information on the original C++ implementation of Recast is available at `https://github.com/memononen/recastnavigation`.

Advanced NavMesh parameters

Now that we know how navigation mesh generations works, let's look at the different parameters you can set to generate them in more detail.

We'll look at how to do these parameters with RAIN using the following steps:

1. Open one of our previous scenes or create a new one with a floor and some blocks for walls.

2. Then, go to **RAIN | Create NavMesh**. Also, right-click on the **RAIN** menu and choose **Show Advanced Settings**. The setup should look something like the following screenshot:

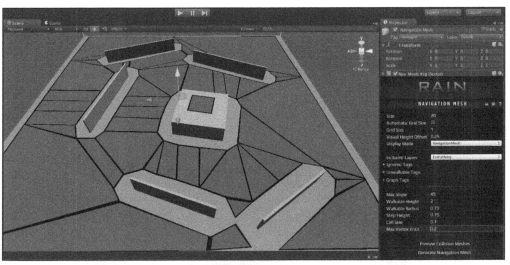

The NavMesh setup

Now let's look at some of the important parameters:

- ○ **Size**: This is the overall size of the navigation mesh. You'll want the navigation mesh to cover your entire level and use this parameter instead of trying to scale up the navigation mesh through the **Scale** transform in the **Inspector** window. For our demo here, set the **Size** parameter to **20**.

- ○ **Walkable Radius**: This is an important parameter to define the character size of the mesh. Remember, each mesh will be matched to the size of a particular character, and this is the radius of the character. You can visualize the radius for a character by adding a Unity **Sphere Collider** script to your object (by going to **Component** | **Physics** | **Sphere Collider**) and adjusting the radius of the collider.

- ○ **Cell Size**: This is also a very important parameter. During the voxel step of the Recast algorithm, this sets the size of the cubes to inspect the geometry. The smaller the size, the more detailed and finer the mesh, but the longer the processing time for Recast. A large cell size makes computation fast but loses detail.

For example, here is a NavMesh from our demo with a cell size of **0.01**:

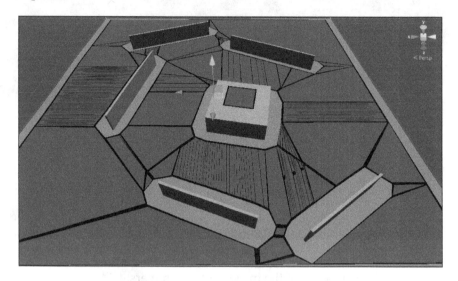

You can see the finer detail here. The following is the navigation mesh generated with a cell size of **0.1**:

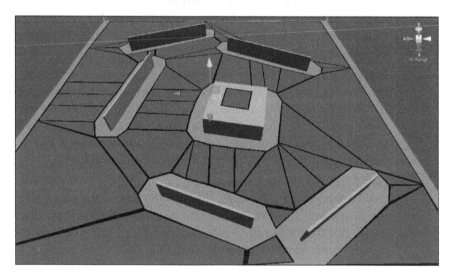

Note the difference between the two screenshots. In the former, walking through the two walls lower down in our picture is possible, but in the latter with a larger cell size, there is no path even though the character radius is the same. Problems like this become greater with larger cell sizes. The following is a navigation mesh with a cell size of **1**:

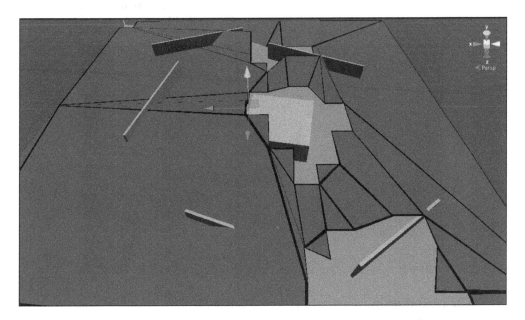

As you can see, the detail becomes jumbled and the mesh itself becomes unusable. With such differing results, the big question is how large should a cell size be for a level? The answer is that it depends on the required result. However, one important consideration is that as the processing time to generate one is done during development and not at runtime, even if it takes several minutes to generate a good mesh then it can be worth it to get a good result in the game.

 Setting a small cell size on a large level can cause mesh processing to take a significant amount of time and consume a lot of memory. It is a good practice to save the scene before attempting to generate a complex navigation mesh.

The **Size, Walkable Radius,** and **Cell Size** parameters are the most important parameters when generating the navigation mesh, but there are more that are used to customize the mesh further:

- **Max Slope**: This is the largest slope that a character can walk on. This is how much a piece of geometry that is tilted can still be walked on. If you take the wall and rotate it, you can see it is walkable:

  The preceding is a screenshot of a walkable object with a slope.

- **Step Height**: This is how high a character can step from one object to another. For example, if you have steps between two blocks, as shown in the following screenshot, this would define how far in height the blocks can be apart and whether the area is still considered walkable:

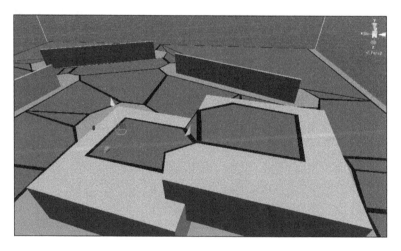

This is a screenshot of the navigation mesh with the step height set to connect adjacent blocks.

- **Walkable Height**: This is the vertical height that is needed for the character to walk. For example, in the previous screenshot, the second block is not walkable underneath because of the walkable height. If you raise it to at least one unit off the ground and set the walkable height to **1**, the area underneath would become walkable:

You can see a screenshot of the navigation mesh with the walkable height set to allow going under the higher block.

These are the most important parameters. There are some other parameters related to the visualization and to cull objects. We will look at culling more in the next section.

Culling areas

Being able to set up areas as walkable or not is an important part of creating a level. To demo this, let's divide the level into two parts and create a bridge between the two. Take our demo and duplicate the floor and pull it down. Then transform one of the walls to a bridge. Then, add two other pieces of geometry to mark areas that are dangerous to walk on, like lava.

Here is an example setup:

This is a basic scene with a bridge to cross.

If you recreate the navigation mesh now, all the geometry will be covered and the bridge won't be recognized. To fix this, you can create a new tag called Lava and tag the geometry under the bridge with it. Then, in the navigation meshes' RAIN component, add Lava to the unwalkable tags. If you then regenerate the mesh, only the bridge is walkable. This is a screenshot of a navigation mesh with polygons that are under the bridge culled out::

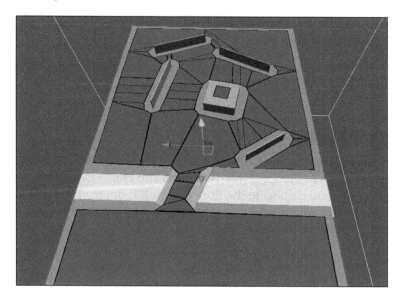

To see this in action, create a new ship and add a target to the scene on different sizes of the bridge. Set the ship's behavior tree to have a **move** node with the target, as shown in the following screenshot:

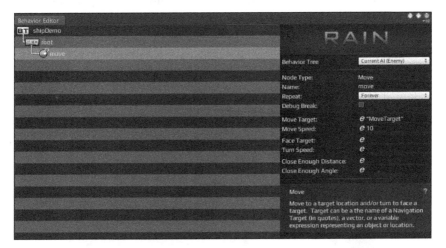

The preceding screenshot shows a basic **move** node to a navigation point behavior tree.

If you run the demo now, you will see the ship cross the bridge:

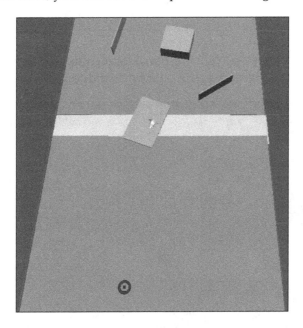

The preceding screenshot shows the ship crossing the bridge to go to its navigation target. Using layers and the walkable tag, you can customize navigation meshes.

Multiple navigation meshes

So far, we have only looked at setting up a single navigation mesh in a scene, but navigation meshes are designed to be per character and not just one for the entire scene. We need multiple navigation meshes, but there is no field to directly set which navigation mesh to use for a character. Instead, RAIN uses a field called **graph tags** to correlate meshes with characters. To see how this works, let's add a second bridge to our scene that is larger and a second ship with double the scale. Here is an example setup:

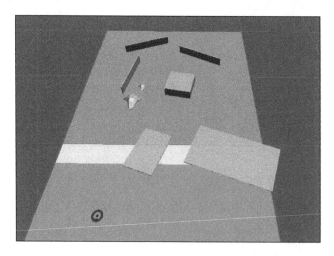

This is a demo scene setup with an additional larger ship and larger bridge. Regenerating the mesh gives us a path over both bridges:

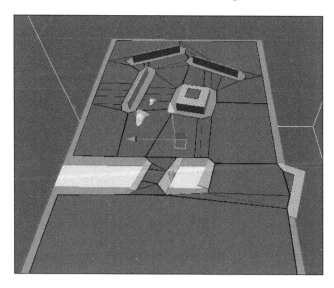

This is a navigation mesh with a smaller walkable radius that can cross both bridges.

Any character using this mesh will be able to go across either bridge. For our larger character to not be able to cross the smaller bridge, we need to generate another mesh with a smaller **Walkable Radius**. Create a second navigation mesh in the scene (**RAIN | Create NavMesh**). Rename the first navigation mesh to `Navigation Mesh Small` and the new one to `Navigation Mesh Large`. In the large one, set the **Walkable Radius** parameter to **1.75**. Generate this mesh and see how it goes over the second bridge but not the first:

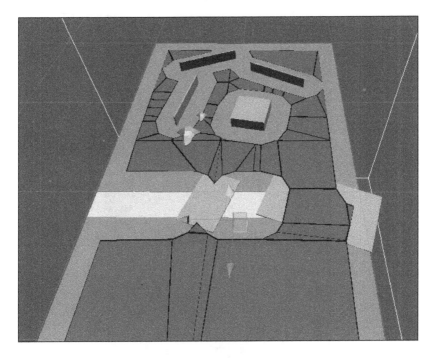

It is a navigation mesh with a larger walkable radius that can cross one bridge.

Then, to match the meshes with the characters for `Navigation Mesh Small`, make sure that you are in **Advanced Settings** and in **Graph Tags**, add an element called `Small Ship`.

The following is a screenshot of a navigation mesh with a graph tag:

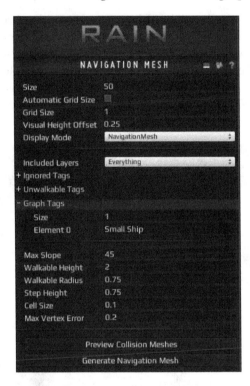

Do the same for `Navigation Mesh Large` with the **Graph Tags** field set to `Large Ship`. Then, for the smaller ship character AI, go to the **Navigator** tab and set its **Graph Tags** field to `Small Ship`:

This is a ship navigator with a graph tag setup.

Do the same with **Graph Tags** for larger ships. With the graph tags matched, if you run the demo now, the larger ship will not take the smaller bridge and go through the smaller one:

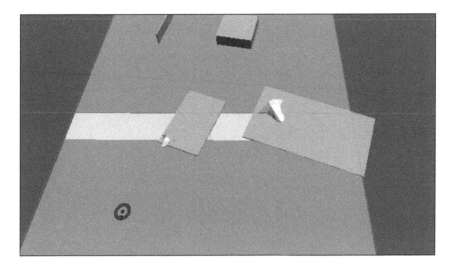

This is a demo with two ships. Only the larger ship can cross the larger bridge.

Summary

Navigation meshes are an important part of game AI. In this chapter, we looked at the different parameters to customize navigation meshes. We looked at things such as setting the character size and walkable slopes and discussed the importance of the cell size parameter. We then saw how to customize our mesh by tagging different areas as not walkable and how to set up multiple navigation meshes for different characters.

We now have all the essential skills we need to create AI in Unity. We've seen how to have a character move, navigate, and sense other characters in our game scenes as well as how to set up behavior trees to make decisions and integrate animation. We also looked at different AI use cases, such as crowds, driving, and had our characters attack and change behavior based on game events. This covers a lot about AI, but game AI is a huge and much studied topic and there is much more to learn. By doing some searching, you'll find that there are many online articles, textbooks, and conference talks that you can study to make even more advanced AI.

Index

U

Unity test scene
  setting up 107, 108

V

vector fields
  adding, to Fame Crowd Simulation API 63
visual sensor
  properties 70
  setting up, in RAIN 74, 75
visual sensor settings
  viewing 69

W

wandering characters
  setting up, with React AI 50
waypoints
  setting up 110, 111

Thank you for buying
Unity AI Programming Essentials

About Packt Publishing

Packt, pronounced 'packed', published its first book, *Mastering phpMyAdmin for Effective MySQL Management*, in April 2004, and subsequently continued to specialize in publishing highly focused books on specific technologies and solutions.

Our books and publications share the experiences of your fellow IT professionals in adapting and customizing today's systems, applications, and frameworks. Our solution-based books give you the knowledge and power to customize the software and technologies you're using to get the job done. Packt books are more specific and less general than the IT books you have seen in the past. Our unique business model allows us to bring you more focused information, giving you more of what you need to know, and less of what you don't.

Packt is a modern yet unique publishing company that focuses on producing quality, cutting-edge books for communities of developers, administrators, and newbies alike. For more information, please visit our website at www.packtpub.com.

Writing for Packt

We welcome all inquiries from people who are interested in authoring. Book proposals should be sent to author@packtpub.com. If your book idea is still at an early stage and you would like to discuss it first before writing a formal book proposal, then please contact us; one of our commissioning editors will get in touch with you.

We're not just looking for published authors; if you have strong technical skills but no writing experience, our experienced editors can help you develop a writing career, or simply get some additional reward for your expertise.

Unity 4.x Game AI Programming

Unity 4.x Game AI Programming

ISBN: 978-1-84969-340-0   Paperback: 232 pages

Learn and implement game AI in Unity3D with a lot of sample projects and next-generation techniques to use in your Unity3D projects

1. A practical guide with step-by-step instructions and example projects to learn Unity3D scripting.

2. Learn pathfinding using A* algorithms as well as Unity3D pro features and navigation graphs.

3. Implement finite state machines (FSMs), path following, and steering algorithms.

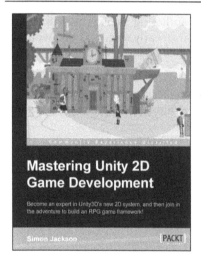

Mastering Unity 2D Game Development

Mastering Unity 2D Game Development

ISBN: 978-1-84969-734-7   Paperback: 474 pages

Become an expert in Unity3D's new 2D system, and then join in the adventure to build an RPG game framework!

1. Learn the advanced features of Unity 2D to change and customize games to suit your needs.

2. Discover tips and tricks for Unity2D's new toolset.

3. Understand scripting, deployment, and platform integration with an example at each step.

Please check **www.PacktPub.com** for information on our titles

Unity 4 Game Development HOTSHOT

ISBN: 978-1-84969-558-9   Paperback: 466 pages

Develop spectacular gaming content by exploring and utilizing Unity 4

1. Understand the new 2D Sprite and Immediate Mode GUI system (OnGUI()/GUI class) in Unity 4, and the difference between 2D and 3D worlds, with clear instruction and examples.

2. Learn about Mecanim System, AI programming, editor script, and Character Controller programming including scripting and how to adapt it to your needs.

3. Create a Menu for an RPG Game—Add Powerups, Weapons, and Armor.

Unity 4.x Game Development by Example: Beginner's Guide

ISBN: 978-1-84969-526-8   Paperback: 572 pages

A seat-of-your-pants manual for building fun, groovy little games quickly with Unity 4.x

1. Learn the basics of the Unity 3D game engine by building five small, functional game projects.

2. Explore simplification and iteration techniques that will make you more successful as a game developer.

3. Take Unity for a spin with a refreshingly humorous approach to technical manuals.

Please check **www.PacktPub.com** for information on our titles

www.ingramcontent.com/pod-product-compliance
Lightning Source LLC
Chambersburg PA
CBHW060143060326
40690CB00018B/3960